How to Make Money Without Money

Without Money

*The Art of Transferable Letters of Credit
and Assignments of Proceeds*

How to Make Money Without Money

The Art of Transferable Letters of Credit and Assignments of Proceeds

Jacob Katsman

CONTINENTAL

C

PUBLISHING

Toronto London Moscow Hong Kong

Continental Publishing
2727 Steeles Ave. W., Suite 301
Toronto, Ontario, Canada
M3J 3G9
www.ccex.org

Cover designed by Jacob Katsman and Kendall Kiddie

Photograph of author by Michael Belenky

Edited by Frances Mundy

Layout by Unified Communications Ltd.

First Edition

ISBN: 0-9683198-0-7

Printed in Canada

Disclaimer: the author and publisher specifically disclaim any responsibility for any liability, loss, or risk, personal or otherwise, which is
incurred as a consequence, directly or indirectly, of the use and application of any of the contents of this book. Living on the threshold of
the 21st Century, the age of the Internet and wireless communications, information is always changing. Keeping abreast of the legal
requirements for export and import in the countries where the company is trading is the responsibility of the trader.

This book is dedicated to
Boris Katsman,
my father, partner, and friend.

CONTENTS

CHAPTER III
Standby Letters of Credit and Performance Bonds

CHAPTER IV
Trader's Know How

CHAPTER V
Case Studies

CHAPTER VI
How to Check Incoming Letters of Credit & Prepare Documents for the Bank

CHAPTER VII

CHAPTER VIII

EPILOGUE

FOREWORD

After having spent more than twenty years in various areas of retail and corporate banking for Den Danske Bank, Denmark, and the Mercantile Bank of Canada, I was introduced to international trade in a big way in 1984 when I was given the task of rewriting all of Mercantile's international trade finance policies and procedures. A few years later, I joined my present employer, Royal Bank of Canada, as Head of the Letters of Credit Department in Toronto. I can say without doubt that there is no more fascinating aspect to banking than that of international trade. It never gets to be routine; almost every day something different occurs, and one deals with a very diverse group of people as well as international counterparties.

I was indeed honoured and pleased when Jacob Katsman asked me to take a look at his new book, *How to Make Money Without Money: The Art of Transferable Letters of Credit and Assignments of Proceeds.* I found the book to be clear, concise, and easy to read. It is free of technical jargon that would make it difficult to understand for all but the most experienced International Trader or Financier. I believe this book will be of great interest to individuals entering the export or import markets. It looks at both in a balanced way. Even international traders with many years of experience may find some useful hints in this book, particularly if they have not taken full advantage of some of the techniques Mr. Katsman describes. In addition the book will serve as an excellent introduction to new bank staff entering the field of Trade Finance.

Rolf Andersen
Trade and Commodity Finance
Royal Bank of Canada

ACKNOWLEDGEMENTS

I would like to thank my mother who taught me the most valuable lesson of all, how to create something out of nothing. Nothing, meaning a simple idea, a seed planted in one's mind; something, meaning a fulfilment of this idea. If you really want something to happen, you must first create a detailed image of it in your mind in full colour and before going to bed at night imagine how you are going to bring this idea to reality. At first you may not have all the answers but with time you will find them one by one. Concepts which are difficult to understand and even foreign will become easy, natural, and eventually, a part of you. This is not magic and does not happen overnight; but, by taking action on carefully planned ideas that have become a reality in your mind, it is only a matter of time before they manifest themselves in the material world.

I also want to thank Antoine Lolas, Rolf Andersen, and Harry Htut of the Royal Bank of Canada in Toronto who were the first people to introduce me to documentary credits. Due to their expert advice I was able to complete my first transferable credit and assignments of proceeds. Your patience was unsurpassed. Special thanks to Gerry Gross and Olga Cooper of Mees Pierson, London, for their consultation and last minute advice.

Professor Bernie Frolic, my teacher in University and dear friend, thank you for urging me on to continue with postgraduate studies. That first paper on "Business Opportunities in the USSR" was the beginning of a great relationship.

I must mention Yakov A. Shabad who has been an inspiration for me all my life. Arguments with Shabad would usually end with him saying, "What will happen after?" No matter what I would answer he would pose the same question again and again until I said, "I do not know, I have to go through stage one to learn the outcome before I can tell you what will happen after." Shabad would be satisfied with such an answer and I would be left with many things to prove.

Elina Katsman, Oleg and Michael Belenky, thank you for your encouragement throughout this project. Frances Mundy, your diligent work and dedication in editing this book are greatly appreciated. David Jack, Mabel Keung, and Irene Shek, you have made unrealistic deadlines possible. Nikolai Pachnev, a special thanks to you for editing the graphics for the Trader's Handbook and for being there with me every step of the way.

I dedicate this book to my father. I will never forget that summer day of 1987 when he called me from a business trip to Belgium and said, "drop whatever you are doing and go find out what a letter of credit is." At the time I was attending York University in Toronto, applying to law school, working part-time as a real estate agent, and editing a community newspaper. How could I drop all of that, I thought at the time: two months later I was fully occupied with international trade. Patrick Wilcox wrote, "Obstacles are those frightful things you see when you take your eyes off your goals." After ten years of sleepless nights, travelling all over the world, meeting interesting people, and moving thousand of tons of a variety of products across the globe, I thank my father for opening the door to the real world and guiding me through the obstacles that lay ahead.

Jacob Katsman

INTRODUCTION

What would you do if you had a million dollars? Would you buy a new house or a car, go on a world tour, or perhaps donate it to a charitable institution? Most likely you would invest in stocks and bonds, mutual funds, or a business that would bring you a regular return on investment. It is not difficult to make money when you have money. The real challenge is, how to make money without money? This book is devoted to answering that question.

In simple language the author brings to light ways to use someone else's money to make money through a thorough knowledge of documentary credit transactions. The book focuses on practical aspects of international trade and banking and teaches the reader the most basic and the more complicated aspects of letters of credit. It is both a how-to manual and a resource book.

Chapter 1 describes the ins and outs of "the contract," the critical first step in the transaction. Incoterms, such as Ex-Works, FOB, and CIF, and letters of credit are introduced.

Chapter 2 provides the crucial information necessary to make money without money. Practical uses of transferable letters of credit, assignments of proceeds, and back-to-back credits are outlined and explained.

Chapter 3 brings to light various uses of standby letters of credit and performance bonds and gives examples showing how such documents can be structured.

Chapter 4 is true to its title "Trader's Know How." It compiles information about international marketing, exclusive rights, foreign exchange, and other pertinent aspects of the trading business. In this chapter, the risks of selling FOB are discussed in great detail and suggestions of ways to minimize them are presented.

The case studies in Chapter 5 give a taste of what it is like to trade and provide the reader with examples of other trader's mistakes. The first case study, "Telephones from Hong Kong to Russia," shows how to use an independent quality inspection certificate in the letter of credit to protect the company against claims. The second, "The Vessel Named Yick Fat," describes the use of performance bonds. The third case study, "Exclusive Rights," explains how a Canadian trading company made millions through establishing exclusive rights to sell Belgian brick-making machines in the former Soviet Union.

Chapter 6 presents checklists for the seller after the documentary credit issuance and upon submission of documents to the bank. This part of the book presents actual shipping documents such as bills of lading, commercial invoices, certificates of origin, and others in a point by point format. For newcomers to international trade, this chapter will be a most valuable asset.

Chapter 7 is the actual text of UCPDC 500 as published by the International Chamber of Commerce. As this document provides the laws and regulations of letters of credit that the banks rely upon when checking documents, UCPDC 500 is reprinted in its entirety to enable the reader to have a complete reference guide within the confines of this book.

Chapter 8 is a glossary of technical terms used in documentary credits, shipping, and banking in general. This chapter will help readers familiarize themselves with the language used in the trade.

The Epilogue introduces Continental Commodity Exchange and briefly describes the impact of electronic commerce on international trade.

In essence the book not only teaches how to use transferable letters of credit and assignments of proceeds, but provides a manual for the international trading business. It gives the reader the most valuable asset of all: Power of Knowledge.

Chapter I

CONTRACTS AND DOCUMENTARY CREDITS

The lips of wisdom are closed, except to the ears of Understanding.

— The Kybalion

CONTRACTS

As a first step in exporting or importing, there must be some type of contract between the buyer and seller stipulating the rights and responsibilities of each party. Should any conflict arise later between the two, reference is generally made to the sales contract in an effort to resolve the misunderstanding. Therefore, it is important that the contract be negotiated with care, so that both buyer and seller are willing and able to function within its terms and know clearly and unambiguously what is expected of them.

Importers and exporters should be aware that many conflicts between buyers and sellers can be traced back to an incomplete or poorly written contract. Arguments and litigation between customer and supplier seldom benefit either, and legal expenses incurred during a court case are often exorbitant. Moreover, the time and effort required by litigation is draining and diverts the trader from his main business activities. Even if a court case is settled in favour of one party or the other, the ultimate result may be the loss of a customer or valuable source of supply. Not even the party in whose favour a court rules may benefit in the long run. The goal, therefore, should be to clearly establish the duties and rights of both parties from the beginning so that any chance of conflict is minimized.

The creation of sales contract can occur in a number of ways:

A potential buyer sends an inquiry to the supplier via fax, e-mail, telex, or other means asking for prices, qualities, and terms of sale. The supplier may furnish the requested information and, at the same time, make an offer to sell a specified quantity of goods at a fixed price and under other stipulated conditions.

A potential seller, knowing that another party is interested in the product, may submit an offer to sell at specified terms and conditions. A buyer who is already familiar with the price and other terms under which a seller is willing to ship may submit a formal order for a specified quantity of goods at a stated price.

An offer to sell or an order requesting shipment is usually already legally binding for the party making the offer or placing the order. Therefore, it is important that an order or offer contain full details concerning the merchandise, including its grade and quality, price, terms of sale, delivery date, and other necessary information. Experienced sellers often put a conditional clause in their offers — for example, this offer is subject to prior sale — therefore leaving themselves an out in case a better price is achievable from another buyer or another situation arises which would prompt such action.

Once a formal offer to buy or sell has been made, it is up to the other party to come up with an appropriate response. If all the terms outlined in the offer are satisfactory, the response might be a formal acceptance. Alternatively, some or all of the conditions may not be acceptable, giving rise to further correspondence or face-to-face negotiation.

Once a seller's written offer has been formally accepted by the buyer, a sales contract is in effect. A sales contract may also come into existence as the result of an order by a buyer. If the seller agrees with the specifications in the order and thinks he can comply with all the provisions, the seller may send a written and signed acknowledgement, thereby again completing a sales contract that is binding on both parties.

Sales contracts, in their simplest form, are merely accepted orders or offers that may arise through correspondence between buyer and seller. For large, complicated sales, however, a <u>detailed contract</u> must be carefully drawn up. Lawyers would advise that the original contract should bear the authorized signatures of both parties. Nevertheless many contracts are signed over a fax machine with a clause in the contract stating, "<u>Fax signature on contract is binding.</u>"

Verbal Contract

The simplest type of contract is a verbal one. Typically, the buyer and seller meet face-to-face and discuss the basic conditions of sale. Having reached a mutually satisfactory agreement, they shake hands to indicate their agreement and willingness to live up to the terms negotiated. Often a face to face meeting is not even necessary; a buyer may simply telephone a supplier to place the order. The latter takes the buyer's verbal promise to accept delivery as sufficiently binding to make shipment.

For a verbal sales contract to be acceptable, there must be a great deal of trust and confidence between buyer and seller. Moreover, the transaction involved must be relatively simple in its terms and specifications. If there is any complexity at all, it may be difficult for the buyer and seller to remember the terms upon which they agreed. Misunderstandings and differences in interpretation can easily arise. One of the parties to the transaction may feel that the other has committed a breach and, as a result, does not feel obligated to fulfil his or her part of the contract. Because the original conditions were not put into writing, the actual agreement can never be accurately determined.

Despite the shortcomings, there are still many situations where verbal contracts are appropriate. When a buyer and seller have had many years of mutually satisfactory dealings of a fairly repetitive nature and, therefore, a great degree of trust and confidence exists between them, a verbal repeat order may be adequate. Traders who buy and sell foreign currencies, for instance, do all their business over the telephone. A purchase and sale is finalized by a verbal agreement between two exchange traders who may never have met face-to-face. Confirmation of the deal is made in writing only after the fact.

As a general rule, when a verbal agreement has been made, it is a good idea to confirm it in writing. This way the underlying agreement is reaffirmed and any misunderstandings can usually be brought into the open before irreparable damage has been done.

Written Contract

In international trade a sales contract comes into existence through a chain of correspondence between the exporter and importer. The importer may come in with an initial inquiry requesting a price quotation for a certain type and quantity of merchandise. The seller, in turn, responds with the desired information. Usually, this response can already be interpreted as an offer that is binding on the exporter.

The point at which correspondence actually becomes a binding contract is sometimes difficult to determine. Courts have ruled, however, that a binding agreement can be represented by a file of correspondence (including telegraphic messages) between the two parties, even though a final agreement on all points between the buyer and seller may never have been explicitly spelled out.

Many firms have pre-printed order and offer forms which, when accepted, become contracts. This greatly simplifies buying and selling procedures in that details that are the same for most contracts of a particular firm need not be specifically typed each time. Major provisions are included in the pre-printed part of the form and variable provisions are typed in as required. A pre-printed form should be examined carefully. In most cases, such a form indicates the party who prepared it has had sufficient time to consider and insert terms and conditions which provide more protective measures for their side.

Problems may arise with a pre-printed form because its fine print tends to favour the party who has issued it. If the other party merely accepts the provisions without attempting to negotiate more favourable terms, that party may be disadvantaged if there is a conflict.

With initial orders, or when large amounts of money are involved, the completion of a sales contract may be too complicated for the use of short forms. At best, there is a great deal of correspondence between buyer and seller before agreement can be reached on the final document. When major purchases such as entire industrial plants are involved, correspondence will not be adequate. Most likely, the buyer and seller, as well as their respective lawyers and technical experts, will have to sit down together for several days or weeks of bargaining before all desired terms and conditions can be incorporated into a mutually acceptable document. In such cases, all technical details must be outlined. Often the contract is accompanied by blueprints and detailed tolerance and performance specifications. If specifications concerning quality, tolerances, performance, or delivery are not met, the contract often provides for remedies or penalties to be paid by the seller. The net result of including all these specifications and details may well be a sales contract that, together with all appendices and schedules, is as voluminous as an entire book.

Whether dealing through correspondence, a pre-printed form, or a long form, there are certain key provisions that every sales contract should contain to avoid ambiguity and possible future conflicts. These include:

5

- Names and addresses of buyer and seller
- Description of goods, including price, weight, grade, and quantity specifications
- Shipping and delivery instructions and required documentation
- Insurance coverage necessary while goods are in transit and designation of the party responsible for costs
- Payment terms and instructions

Other optional provisions might specify:

- Method of packaging
- Method of marking
- Inspections and tests allowed by the buyer before delivery
- Warranties of the seller concerning the quality and/or performance of the product
- Provisions for bid and performance bonds or guarantees
- Remedies allowed by either party in case of default by the other
- Means of arbitration of disputes or claims that may arise
- Definition of jurisdiction under which any disputes shall be resolved

To avoid possible conflicts about quality, grade, quantity, or price, every effort should be made to describe the goods in the sales contract exactly as buyer and seller intend them to be.

Confusion and misunderstandings over weights and other quantity measures are not uncommon. For example, a ton has a different real weight depending on whether it is a short, metric, or long ton. As these and other quantity terms may be ambiguous, careful definition in the sales contract is important. Terms indicating grades or qualities are frequently harder to define than weights and quantities. A term for defining one particular degree of quality in one country may have a different meaning in another.

When writing a sales contract, international traders should take great care to clearly define their terms and avoid all ambiguous words or abbreviations. Detailed contracts often have, in one of the first articles, a definition of all terms. It may also be possible to clarify the description of goods by reference in the sales contract to catalogue numbers, plans or drawings, engineering specifications, or even samples previously given to the buyer.

Price quotations can also be a source of misunderstanding. The contract should specify the price and terms of sale, that is, FOB Stowed L/S/D (Name of Load Port). When deferred payment terms are offered, an importer may wish to add a premium to the price to cover interest expenses until final payment is received.

Regarding delivery of goods, a contract might provide for no penalty in case of an excusable delay and a fixed or graduated fee for non-excusable delays. An illustrative clause providing for delay penalties might read as follows:

> In the event that the availability for delivery of all or any portion of the contract equipment and materials are delayed for other than excusable causes beyond the delivery date, the seller shall pay to the purchaser actual damages at an equivalent rate of 0.10% of the total contract price per day beyond the stipulated delivery date. In no case shall such payment exceed 5% of the contract price.

When a specific delivery deadline is stated, this generally means that the ocean bill of lading should be dated on or before the stipulated date. To make sure that the goods have actually been put on a vessel on time, the buyer should specifically request an "on-board" bill of lading.

A buyer can provide for the enforcement of a shipping deadline by an appropriate stipulation in a letter of credit. Alternatively, if an importer receives title documents against payment or acceptance of a draft drawn, it is necessary to make sure that the on-board bill of lading is dated on or before the shipping deadline before paying or accepting the draft.

Shipping Documentation

An importer who wishes to claim a shipment at the dock to clear it through customs requires certain shipping documents. The most common of these are bills of lading, commercial invoices, and certificates of origin. It is most important that the importer specify in the sales contract exactly what documentation is required, the number of copies, and the detailed information that is to be included.

In many countries, goods may only be imported if the buyer has previously obtained a valid import license. Without a license, it may be impossible to pass goods through customs and they may be confiscated. The exporter should, therefore, make sure that the sales contract provides for the importer to obtain all necessary licenses. Importers also should make sure that exporters obtain any required licenses. Some countries have limited the quantities of certain goods that may be exported. Once this quantity restriction for any calendar period is reached, no further export licenses may be issued.

Currency

The currency in which payment is due should be clearly specified in the contract. Quotations may be made in the currency of the exporter, importer, or a third country. Often the exporters will prefer a quote in their own currency in order to reduce the foreign exchange risk and to enable them more easily to determine profit. Before accepting payment in the importer's or a third currency, exporters should make sure that payments can readily be converted into their own currency and that their exchange risk can be covered.

Payment Terms

The sales contract should specify the exact payment terms. Terms negotiated in any particular contract depend on competitive practices, the custom in the industry, the financial position and reputation of the buyer, and the buyer's and seller's relative bargaining strength. Terms that may be used include the following:

Cash in Advance. Since the seller receives payment before shipping the goods, this is clearly the most desirable method from the exporter's point of view. From the importers point of view it is least desirable because money is paid in advance and the risk of non-performance is not secured.

Irrevocable Letter of Credit. When the credit is issued by a prime bank of excellent standing or confirmed by a reputable bank, this term is almost as safe from the exporter's point of view as cash in advance. As long as exporters can comply with the documentation specified in the letter of credit within the stipulated time period, in most cases, they can be assured of payment.

Documents Against Payment. Under this payment term, shipping documents are turned over to the importer against payment of a sight draft for the amount due drawn on him by the exporter. Although the exporter or his bank retains control over the shipment until payment is received, there is, nevertheless, a considerable amount of risk for the exporter. The importer may, for instance, simply refuse to accept the shipment. By that time, the goods are usually on the high seas or at a foreign port and can probably not be disposed of except at a reduced price.

Documentary Acceptance. In this case documents are turned over to the importer on acceptance of a time draft drawn on him. The tenure of the draft is for a stipulated period of time such as 30, 60, 90, or 180 days. In addition to all the risks mentioned under documents against payment, an additional danger for the exporter is that the accepted draft may not be paid at maturity.

Consignments. Sometimes the exporter may wish to retain title to the goods while at the same time physically turning them over to the importer to allow the arrangement of sales and deliveries to final customers. This can be achieved by consignment terms. The goods are actually sent to the importer to allow the latter to display and/or warehouse them. Title, however, remains with the exporter. Once the importer has made a final sale, he or she is obliged to pay the consignor (exporter) promptly for the merchandise involved. Clearly, by giving up physical possession of the goods, the exporter runs a substantial risk unless the consignee is of undoubted integrity.

Open Account. In North America the payment term most commonly used is the open account. This is certainly the least cumbersome method. The seller merely ships the goods to the buyer and separately mails the buyer the title documents and invoice calling for payment within a stipulated period of time. Before a seller agrees to ship on open-account terms, it is necessary to ascertain the honesty and financial strength of the buyer. Usually, in domestic transactions, this represents no problem. To get a complete credit history on any particular buyer, the seller merely contacts his local bank. The latter, through its banking relationships, makes contact with a bank, some other financial institution, or a credit agency that has intimate knowledge of the buyer's business, financial strength, reputation, and payment habits. In international trade, open-account terms are usually used only between large companies of undoubted repute and firms having a long history of satisfactory dealings during which a high degree of mutual confidence has been developed.

Packaging and Marking

Proper packaging can be extremely important, depending on the type of product and its destination. Ocean voyages may be most damaging to goods that are not properly packaged. Goods subject to breakage have to be crated, and those subject to moisture damage must be wrapped in plastic. Some products may require some special treatment or coating before shipment, while others have to be refrigerated during transit. The markings of outer and inner boxes are often subject to strict control at the country of destination. Each country has its own regulations regarding, for example, the system of weights and measures to be used to show quantity of content, the language to be used on the boxes, and so on.

Improper packaging and markings may prevent the goods from getting safely to their destination or may cause local customs authorities to either reject the shipment or levy a heavy fine against the consignee. Thus, it is in the best interest of the importer to specify clearly in the sales contract the packaging and marking required. If an exporter does not comply with packing and marking instruction, the importer is justified in refusing to accept the shipment.

Warranties

It is, of course, to the advantage of the buyer to have warranties of the seller included in the contract. If the seller guarantees not only against product defects, but also for proper performance, he may be liable not only for replacing a defective product but also for consequential damages. A clear definition in the contract of exactly what is and is not warrantied is therefore advisable. A typical warranty clause in a contract covering supply of equipment may read as follows:

> The seller shall warrant that the design, material, and workmanship will be of the highest grade and consistent with the established and generally accepted standards for equipment of this type; and that it will be in full conformity with the specification and seller's offer.
>
> The seller agrees that this warranty will survive acceptance of and payment for the equipment, whether any defect shall be patent or latent, for one year after satisfactory full-load operation but not to exceed 30 months after the date of delivery to the port of exit of final shipment under the contract.
>
> The seller's entire obligation under this warranty shall be to repair or, at his option, replace any part of the equipment which, under the specified use and proper maintenance, proves defective within one year from the date of satisfactory full-load operation of the unit concerned.

Performance Guarantee. Sometimes exporters are expected to back up their warranties with bank performance credits (in the form of a standby letter of credit), guarantees, or performance bonds. If delivery or performance does not comply with previously agreed-on specifications, the importer has the right to draw under the guarantee or bond.

Inspection. Sometimes a buyer may wish to have the right to inspect the merchandise or equipment while it is being manufactured. In this case, an inspection clause should be included in the contract. When shipments are made on a documentary-collection basis, the buyer may wish to have the right to inspect the merchandise before accepting or paying the draft. This must also be clearly stipulated in the contract. Moreover, if the goods are defective, the contract should specify whether the buyer may buy them at a reduced price, or if they should be returned to the seller at the latter's expense.

In practice, it is often difficult or impossible for an importer receiving goods on a documents-against-payment basis to inspect them prior to payment. To claim goods from the carrier requires a negotiable bill of lading. To obtain the negotiable bill of lading, however, the importer must first pay for the goods.

Arbitration

If disputes arise between buyer and seller, they can be amicably settled between the parties, taken to court, or settled by arbitration. Unless disputes can be settled directly between the parties, the next best alternative is arbitration. Court procedures tend to be time-consuming and costly, and judges may not always be familiar with the specific practices of the industry and the laws that apply to a particular case.

Arbitration, on the other hand, is often faster and less costly than the courts, and the decision is made by people who are well informed about the practices and problems in the particular industry. The parties can, of course, always agree to arbitration after a dispute arises. It is safer, however, to include an arbitration clause in the sales agreement.

The arbitration clause should specify an arbitration tribunal to which a dispute will be referred. There are many reputable arbitration associations, such as the International Chamber of Commerce, to name one. Some trade associations have their own arbitration tribunals. In addition to the number of arbitrators and their selection, the contract should specify the place where the arbitration is to be held, how the cost of the arbitration is to be divided, and the scope of the arbitration.

INCOTERMS

BEFORE OPENING YOUR MOUTH,
PUT YOUR MIND IN GEAR
Assume always when negotiating with a buyer or supplier that
he or she is smarter and better informed than you. If you
assume for a second that your counterpart is weaker than you
or that you are smarter, you have already lost.
— Dr. Boris Katsman

To help traders communicate with one another, the International Chamber of Commerce (ICC) published a set of rules specifying obligations of buyers and sellers in a contract. Incoterms were first published in 1936 and were most recently updated in 1990 to reflect the modern methods of international trade. (A complete text of ICC Incoterms can be obtained from the ICC Publishers S.A. 38, Course Albert 1ER 75008 Paris Tel: (1) 49.53.28.28 Fax: (1) 42.25.36.23.) Incoterms are accepted by the banks as legal terminology for letter of credit transactions. Incoterms have universal meaning. Without Incoterms traders would spend countless hours answering questions such as whose responsibility will it be to ship the goods, who will pay for insurance of the goods, who will obtain export and import permits, if any, and who will clear the goods through customs, et cetera. With Incoterms a supplier in Hong Kong can tell a buyer in London that the terms of sale are simply CIP or FOB and the other party would automatically understand his or her obligations and agree, disagree, or negotiate terms of sale.

Ex-Works (...Named Place)

"Ex-Works" is the term of sale most suited to the seller. Under the ex-works conditions of the contract the seller only has to make the goods ready for pick-up at his warehouse. The seller is not responsible for loading of the goods on to the container or truck provided by the buyer or clearing the goods for export unless agreed otherwise. More often than not, suppliers do load their merchandise into the buyer's truck or container. The buyer has to arrange for a method of transportation from the seller's warehouse, or works at his own risk and coordinates all further export arrangements.

If the trading company wants to protect its source of supply, it is advisable to structure its purchase contract with a supplier on the ex-works basis. This way the trading company will be responsible for the booking of the container and would make sure that export documentation is showing the trading company's name as shipper on the Bills of Lading, Certificate of Origin, and other export documentation.

If the seller or supplier is responsible for the preparation of export documentation, often the supplier's name, sometimes with full corporate address, telephone, and fax number, will be mentioned somewhere in the documents. As trading companies find themselves in the middle of what can be described as a bridge between the manufacturer in one country and an ultimate buyer (user of goods) or a trader or distributor in another country, information such as the manufacturer's address or phone may prove costly for the trading company's future sales. That same buyer may attempt to bypass the trading company, by dealing directly with the named manufacturer for the next purchase. If there is no exclusive rights agreement between the manufacturer and the trading company, the trading company is always at risk that after an initial sale to a foreign buyer, the foreign buyer may approach the manufacturer directly. The trading company that developed the new export business in the first place will only get a 'thank-you' as remuneration. To protect its source of supply a trader must have the know how of contracts and export documentation. Structuring the deal properly from the start is a vital component to a successful transaction.

F.C.A. Free Carrier (...Named Place)

Under the Free Carrier terms of sale, the seller must deliver the goods and clear the export into the possession of the carrier designated by the buyer at a specific location. If no specific point is indicated by the buyer, the seller may choose within the place or range stipulated where the carrier will deliver the goods into his possession. Provided that the buyer instructs the seller to deliver the goods to a freight forwarder who is not a "carrier," the seller is said to have completed his obligation when the goods are in the forwarder's custody. Under FCA the seller must provide a commercial invoice in accordance with the contract of sale; provide at his own expense an export licence if one is required; bear all risks of damage or loss of goods until they have been delivered into the custody of the carrier, freight forwarder, or other person chosen by the buyer; notify the buyer that the goods have been delivered into the carrier's custody; provide the buyer with documentary proof stating that the goods have been delivered; and pay any costs associated with checking quality, measuring, weighing, and so forth, which are needed for the goods to be delivered to the carrier.

The buyer's responsibilities under FCA terms are to pay for the goods; to obtain at his own risk and expenses any import licence if needed; to take care of all customs formalities; to contract the carriage at his own expense; to take delivery of goods; and to bear the risk of loss of or damage to the cargo from the time that it is delivered. Incoterms set out other responsibilities for the buyers and sellers, most of which are common sense after the main distinctions are made. FCA terms are not as popular as FOB, CIF, or CFR Incoterms among traders.

F.O.B Free On Board (...Named Port of Shipment)

FOB stipulates that the seller of the goods must load the goods into a container, deliver the container to a port, and load it on a vessel. Break bulk cargo has to be taken on board and loaded inside the vessel. The buyer, on the other hand, takes possession of the goods when they pass over the ship's rail at the named port of shipment. The buyer is therefore responsible for all costs and risk of loss of or damage to the cargo from that port. Under the FOB terms, the seller must clear the goods for export. Although FOB terms should only be used for sea or inland waterway transport, they are used for all kinds of transport in the everyday conversations among traders. Under the FOB contract, the seller does not have to pay for freight cost or insurance cost. Rather, this responsibility falls on the buyer. When shipping commodities, FOB terms can be profitable for the

15

buyer if the buyer is chartering a vessel. A good freight rate can usually be negotiated where the buyer is a frequent customer in the freight market. In shipping steel, for example, a $1 - $3 per metric ton saving can be realized by the company chartering the vessel. On a 20,000 metric ton shipment this difference translates into $20,000 - $60,000 profit.

FOB Stowed or FOB ST may often be seen in a commodity contract. Stowed or ST means that the seller is responsible for stowing the goods loaded on board the vessel inside a vessels hall. Furthermore in addition to FOB Stowed, the contract may specify FOB ST L/S/D. The term L/S/D stands for Lashing/Securing/Dunnaging. In this case the seller is also responsible and has to pay for L/S/D.

F.A.S. Free Along Ship (...Named Port of Shipment)

Free Along Ship is very similar to FOB in the responsibilities it assigns to the buyer and seller. FAS means that the seller must deliver the goods alongside the vessel on the quay or in lighters at the designated port of shipment. Again this term can only properly be used for sea or inland waterway transportation and usually is, due to the explicit name of term. Unlike FOB, FAS puts the responsibility on the buyer to clear the goods for export.

The buyer must pay for and arrange the freight and insurance for the contracted cargo. The seller must provide proof of delivery, transport documentation, or an electronic message of the same to the buyer. Other obligations are similar to FOB terms.

C.F.R. Cost and Freight (...Named Port of Destination)

The main feature of CFR terms of sale is that the seller's responsibility includes the arrangement of the freight to bring the goods to an agreed port of destination at his expense. The buyer, however, is responsible for insuring the goods during transportation. It is not mandatory for the buyer to insure the goods, but if something should happen to the goods during transportation the seller could not be held responsible for the damage. After the goods have been delivered on board a vessel, the responsibility is transferred from the seller to the buyer.

Under CFR terms, the seller must clear the goods for export, but once the goods arrive at the port of discharge all duties and taxes are the buyer's responsibility. The seller must provide the buyer with necessary export documents such as a full set of original bills of lading, certificates of origin, commercial invoices, certified if needed, and so forth. CFR terms only apply to sea and inland waterway transport.

In the commodity business the buyer usually prefers to organize the insurance and be the beneficiary of the insurance policy. This control of insurance allows the buyer quicker compensation in the event of cargo damage or loss. Where a letter of credit is involved and the buyer is a trading company acting as an agent, the control of insurance will allow him to insure the cargo for the amount stated in the first letter of credit (L/C), assuming that the first amount is greater than the second amount on the back-to-back L/C or a transfer of the original documentary credit. If the seller were to be responsible for insuring the goods he would generally insure them for the invoice amount, usually less than the value of goods under the first L/C. For a trading company in the middle of a transaction to avoid a discrepancy, the L/C insurance value must correspond to the value requested on the first L/C. If this point is overlooked and the cargo is under-insured, the bank will find a discrepancy in the documents and the trading company will have a difficult time collecting payment from the buyer and honouring its obligation to pay the supplier.

Before the Incoterms were updated in 1990, CFR was called C&F cost and freight. As trading companies still use C&F in their correspondence with each other, it is worth nothing that the terms are exactly the same as under CFR.

C.I.F. Cost Insurance and Freight (...Named Port of Destination)

Unlike CFR which is a new name for C&F, CIF has not changed from the first publication of Incoterms in 1936. Together with FOB, CIF is probably the most frequently used term in the international trade business. The only difference between CFR and CIF is that under CIF terms the seller is responsible for obtaining the insurance for the contractual amount at his own expense. Usually the insurance must cover the full value of the goods plus 10 per cent. The insurance generally covers all risk, including war risk, from the seller's warehouse to the port of discharge only.

CIF requires that the seller clear the goods for export. The buyer should be careful with CIF terms if he is acting as a trading house, that is, in the middle between the supplier and the end buyer, where a letter of credit is involved. As with CFR, where the buyer controls the insurance of the goods, the value on the second L/C will be different from the first L/C unless the trading house or first beneficiary under the L/C is not making any money on the transaction and transfers the L/C at the same face value. Because this is not the case in most transactions, trading houses must be aware of this problem.

A solution can be found by asking the second beneficiary (supplier) to purchase the insurance for more than 10 per cent over the invoice value to match the amount on the first L/C. Doing this may alert the supplier to the amount of profit you, the trading house, are making on the transaction. Nevertheless, if such a situation occurs and you have to have a transferrable L/C this may be only way out. There is however another more expensive solution, which requires buying a spare insurance policy and substituting it during the document negotiation stage with the bank. Some banks will allow for such substitution of documents since you (the first beneficiary) are responsible for presentation of all documents required under the L/C. To avoid such problems from the start, however, it is best to ask for a CFR letter of credit and negotiate the cost of insurance out of the purchase price.

C.P.T. Carriage Paid to and C.I.P. Carriage and Insurance Paid to (…Named Place of Destination)

Similar in function to CFR and CIF, CPT and CIP differ only in that an additional responsibility on the seller's list of duties includes the contracting of carriage from the port of discharge to the named destination (usually the buyer's warehouse or local customs point). Both CPT and CIP terms may be used for any mode of transport including multimodal transport. The risk of the goods being damaged or lost is transferred from the seller to the buyer when the goods are delivered into the custody of the carrier.

"Carrier" is defined as anyone who, in a contract of carriage, performs or procures the act of carriage, by air, rail, road, inland waterway, sea, or by a combination of such modes. If there is more than one carrier, the risk passes when the goods have been delivered to the first carrier. Under CPT and CIP terms the seller must clear the goods for export and the buyer is responsible for clearing local customs at the place of arrival and paying all import duties and taxes, if any.

CIP differs from CPT only in insurance obligation for the goods. Insurance is the seller's responsibility in CIP and the buyer's, in CPT. The insurance must be obtained for inland transportation which may be difficult in high-risk countries where there is an excessive degree of civil unrest, organized criminal activity, political instability, or a combination of these circumstances.

Under CIP terms the seller is only responsible for purchasing insurance for minimum coverage or for the value contractually agreed. CIP is frequently used in container shipments. When a letter of credit is involved and there is no trading company in the middle of the transaction, CIP terms protect both the seller and buyer and reduce the obligations of the buyer to the minimum of clearing local customs. In cases where restricted goods are being exported, such as alcohol, tobacco, or firearms, the seller may only agree to sell on the basis of CFR, CIF, CPT, or CIP in order to control the actual export of product from the country of origin. Due to labelling, packaging, or distribution restrictions certain products cannot be resold in specific markets and therefore the seller will want to control the freight arrangements.

D.A.F. Delivered At Frontier (...Named Port)

D.E.S. Delivered Ex-Ship (...Named Port of Destination)

D.E.Q. Delivered Ex-Quay/Duty Paid (...Named Port of Destination)

D.D.U. Delivered Duty Unpaid (…Named Place of Destination)

D.D.P. Delivered Duty Paid (…Named Place of Destination)

The above-mentioned Incoterms are not as frequently used in international trade as the terms described earlier. They are, nevertheless, useful during initial negotiations with a respective buyer or supplier. If you, a trader, are talking to a supplier that has prior experience in exporting to your specific market, you can ask if he can quote you a price DDP Moscow, for example. There is a good chance that the supplier will not be able to do that, but you will have given the impression of being a professional trader who knows Incoterms.

A complete text of all Incoterms can be obtained from the ICC, a local bank, or a library.

DOCUMENTARY LETTER OF CREDIT

In order to get a loan, you must first prove you don't need it.
—*Vic Oliver*

The documentary letter of credit is a key element in making money without money. You do not need a loan to transfer a letter of credit issued in your favour. Through a documentary credit both the buyer and seller are ensured security for their part of the deal and the trader is secure in the knowledge that he or she will receive payment when the deal is complete.

Textbooks define a letter of credit as an engagement by a bank (issuer) made at the request of a customer (applicant) such that the issuer, independent of the applicant, will honour drafts or other demands for payment upon compliance with the conditions specified in the credit.

Another technical definition explains letters of credit in the following manner:

A letter of credit contains an undertaking by a bank, which in turn is the second step of an agreement between the buyer and seller to pay to a stipulated beneficiary a certain sum of money. Payment is usually made upon the tendering of certain documents, such as bills of lading, inspection certificates, and insurance policies, witnessing full or partial performance.

To understand letters of credit, you should first consider what factors are important to a buyer and a seller when negotiating a contract:

BUYER'S PRIORITIES
- quality/quantity of goods
- delivery on time in the right location
- payment made as late as possible

SELLER'S PRIORITIES
- correct payment amount
- proper currency
- payment received as soon as possible

The **DOCUMENTARY LETTER OF CREDIT** bridges the gap between the buyer and seller by providing a mechanism of security for both parties through which a transaction can flow.

Quality and Quantity - How to be Sure

As a buyer, one way you can be sure of the quality of goods is by requiring the seller to provide a quality certificate, sometimes called a "beneficiaries quality certificate." This is a simple piece of paper on which the seller warrants that the goods are of acceptable quality to the country of origin where the goods are produced. When the supplier is a world class company that values its reputation, such a certificate may be sufficient. However, in cases where the supplier's reputation is unknown or is in question, a quality certificate issued by an independent organization should be requested. Societe General de Surveillance, better known as SGS, is a world-recognized organization which offers a variety of services, one of which is testing products for quality and quantity. SGS follows specific guidelines and test procedures. For example, on a shipment of 336 televisions, an SGS inspector may remove 50 televisions from their boxes, plug them into the electrical outlet and test them for sharpness of picture and other interior and exterior features. SGS inspection will vary in complexity depending on the requirements of the party paying for the inspection.

On receiving a request for inspection, a surveyor will ask what degree of testing is required. Accordingly, he or she may then perform a chemical analysis on the goods or simply verify the test certificates and take the data shown on the certificates as factual. In either case, the surveyor should give an accurate report as to the amount of testing done and the results of such testing. Survey companies may also be employed to perform a draft survey and then present a report as to the quantity of the goods loaded on board a particular vessel. Or they may designate an inspector to tally the exact quantity loaded.

An important consideration is who will pay for the inspection. Inspections of quality and quantity may range from $400 to $6,000 depending on the country where the inspection is performed, the product, and the quantity. The buyer may want the seller to pay for the inspection in order to save money. However this saving may not prove to be in the buyer's interest because any defects or shortages will be first reported to the party paying for the inspection, in this case the supplier.

Correct Time and Place of Delivery

As a buyer you want to be sure that the goods you bought are delivered before a specific date and to the right place (warehouse, port, city, country). In the structure of a letter of credit there is a section called Latest Shipment Date. This section sets up a provision by which a seller must ship the goods ordered under the letter of credit before a specified date, for example, March 30, 1998. If for some reason the goods are not shipped before March 30, 1998 then there will be a discrepancy in the letter of credit and the seller may not be able to collect money from the letter of credit. The document evidencing latest shipment is usually a Bill of Lading, or other transport document.

The Bill of Lading is usually issued by a carrier or agent of a named shipping company confirming the quantity of goods loaded on board or inside a container, and the shipment date. The bill of lading also states the loading port, discharge port, consignee, and notify party. The Bills of Lading are usually issued in three originals, called a "full set."

Documents Presented Under a Letter of Credit

The documents usually presented under the letter of credit include those relating to proof of shipment and delivery. They are presented in the original unless otherwise specified and must conform in all material respects to the credit terms. These documents include the invoice, bills of lading, insurance policies, certificates of inspection, and other documents as required. Once tendered, these documents serve for the benefit of the customer and as security in the hands of the bank against reimbursement to the bank by the customer.

The invoice constitutes one of the principal documents witnessing the underlying transaction, its counterpart being the purchase order. The terms of sale used in the invoice should confirm precisely the order of the customer. The description of goods in the letter of credit has to be repeated word for word in the commercial invoice in order for the invoice to comply with credit terms. The Uniform Customs and Practice for Documentary Credits provides certain guidelines respecting the drafting and adequacy of invoices, and unless otherwise specified in the letter of credit, commercial invoices must be made out in the name of the applicant. Banks may refuse invoices issued for amounts in excess of the amount permitted by the credit. Although the description of the goods in the invoice must correspond exactly with the description in the credit, in all other documents, the goods may be described in general terms consistent with the description of the goods in the credit. If the credit uses the words 'about' or 'circa' in connection with the amount or quantity or unit price of the goods, the invoice may show a difference of up to 10 per cent more or less. Unless the credit stipulates that the quantity of goods specified must not be exceeded or reduced, a tolerance of up to 5 per cent more or less is permitted, but this does not apply when the credit specifies quantity in terms of a stated number of packing units or individual items. The amount of the invoice must not exceed the initial limit unless a tolerance for that amount is stated in the credit.

The most important document under a letter of credit is the original bill of lading, usually issued in three originals along with additional non-negotiable copies. A bill of lading is a negotiable title document because the holder of the full set of original bills of lading has control of the goods. The bills of lading can be consigned directly to the buyer, to the order of the issuing bank, or to order blank endorsed, depending on the arrangement between the buyer, seller, and the issuing bank.

To be more certain of compliance by beneficiary (seller), the applicant (buyer) may require the beneficiary to present certificates of origin, weight, quality, and analysis, to name a few. The least reliable certificate is one that the beneficiary himself is required to issue, even if in the form of an affidavit. More reliance can of course be placed on a certificate issued by an independent inspection and testing agency, or better yet, an agent qualified in the field and known to the customer.

If the credit stipulates that a certificate of origin is required, and no further definition is given, the issuing bank is entitled to accept such a certificate as presented. This means that it is not required to determine whether the issuer of the certificate was a body independent of the beneficiary, or what the exact circumstances of the inspection or attestation giving rise to the certificate were. Furthermore, the issuing bank is not required to demand in a certificate of origin, details about the shipment other than the origin. The certificate of origin must relate to other documents presented under a letter of credit as to the description of goods, exporter's/shipper's name, consignee, and notify party unless otherwise specified in the special conditions of a letter of credit.

In examining the certificates, the bank looks to the title of the document, the date, the place of issue, the person or body issuing the certificate, as well as the description of goods, all of which must be compatible with the elements set out in the letter of credit. Bankers tend to skim over chemical or technical descriptions of the composition of the goods unless the credit requires an attestation of the presence of a percentage of a certain chemical composition, a specific packaging, or the size of the product.

UCPDC 500, reprinted in full in Chapter 7, describes in detail rules and regulations the banks use to check documents presented under a letter of credit. It is very important to understand the rules of UCPDC 500 prior to issuing or accepting a documentary credit.

Payment for the Goods Under a Letter of Credit

Letter of credit terms allow for sight payment and term payments. Payment at sight means that the beneficiary should receive from his bank 100 per cent of the payment under the given letter of credit within a few days after the presentation of conforming documents. Depending on how the payment clause is structured, the time of actual payment may vary from three to five banking days, or later, if the applicant's bank is required to check documents prior to affecting payment.

With term payments, the beneficiary may receive payment within 30 to 360 days after the presentation of conforming documents under the credit to the negotiating bank (usually the beneficiary's bank). The deferred payment depends on payment terms as specified in the sales contract.

Payment terms from the buyer's perspective.

A buyer should attempt to arbitrate that the documents under a given letter of credit (L/C) be negotiated at the counters of the issuing bank. If the L/C specifies this, then the seller's bank must forward all documents to the buyer's bank for negotiation.

The seller's banker still has the responsibility to check documents for discrepancies and to advise the issuing bank if any have been found. If discrepancies are found and they cannot be remedied, then it is up to the issuing bank and the buyer afterwards to determine whether or not the documents will be accepted as presented. If discrepancies are typographical in nature and the goods are delivered in the precise specification as ordered, there may not be any problems. Nevertheless, as a seller you never want to be in such a position. If L/C documents have discrepancies, even minor, never assume that the buyer will accept them and your product thereafter. The buyer may refuse to take delivery of the goods and withhold payment using discrepant documents as excuse.

Payment terms from the seller's perspective.

A seller should attempt to negotiate that payment under a letter of credit allow reimbursement by tested telex (T/T Reimbursement Allowed). This allows the advising/negotiating bank (seller's bank) to claim reimbursement via T/T as soon as the documents are found to be in conformity with the terms and conditions of the L/C at their counters. The seller will therefore usually receive payment within three to five working days after the telex claiming reimbursement is sent. If the seller's bank finds discrepancies in documents presented, it will always allow the seller to put the documents in order prior to notifying the issuing bank.

The financial strength of the bank issuing a letter of credit should also be examined, and if necessary, a credit may have to be confirmed.

Confirmation charges vary from bank to bank and are adjusted depending on the country of origin of the letter of credit, the currency stipulated, and its amount. Some banks may refuse to confirm letters of credit issued by banks in countries with high political risk. In case the credit is not confirmed and T/T reimbursement is allowed, the seller's bank will credit the account of its client upon receipt of funds from the reimbursing bank.

Application for Documentary Credit

1. Reference Number _____ Date of Expiry_____

2. Please issue
    ( ) Irrevocable Documentary   ( ) By Airmail
    ( ) Revocable Credit   ( ) By Cable - Full Particulars
    ( ) Transferable   which will be the operative
                                      credit instrument

3. For Account of (Applicant) - [Full name and address]

4. In Favour of (Beneficiary) - [Full name and address]

5. Advising Bank - [Full name and address]

6. Currency and Amount
    ( ) Maximum   ( ) Approximately

7. Partial shipments   Transhipment
    ( ) Allowed   ( ) Allowed
    ( ) Not Allowed   ( ) Not Allowed

8. Available by
    ( ) Drafts   ( ) at sight   ( ) at _____ days sight
    ( ) at _____ days_____   ( ) deferred payment

9. For 100% of invoice value (unless otherwise indicated) drawn at your option on you or your correspondent.

10. Shipment/Despatch/Taking in charge from/At _____

No later than _____

11. For Transportation to _____

Accompanied by the following documents (In duplicate unless otherwise indicated.) Indicate by an "X"

12. ( ) Commercial Invoice

13. ( ) Customs Invoice, if required, in Quintuplicate or_____ copies

14. a) ( ) Full set clean "ON BOARD" Marine Bills of Lading, made out to order, blank endorsed and marked:
   ( ) Freight prepaid   ( ) Freight collect   ( ) Notify applicant
   (State if otherwise)

   b) ( ) Combined Transport/Forwarder's Cargo Receipt/ Forwarder's Bill of Lading/House Bill of Lading (Delete items not applicable), made out to order, blank endorsed and marked:
   ( ) Freight prepaid   ( ) Freight collect   ( ) Notify applicant

15. ( ) Air waybill marked:
   ( ) Freight prepaid   ( ) Freight collect   ( ) Consigned to applicant

16. ( ) Insurance Policy/Certificate in negotiable form, covering Institute Cargo clauses "ALL RISKS", Institute war, S.R.C.C. and T.P.N.D. clauses for_____% of invoice value.

17. ( ) Packing List

18. ( ) Certificate of original indicating _____ origin

   Other Documents
   ( )
   ( )
   ( )

19. Covering (Brief description of merchandise)

20. Terms of delivery
    ( ) F.O.B.   ( )C.F.R .   ( )C.I.F.   ( ) Other_____

21. Special conditions

    All Banking charges outside of Applicant's country for
    ( ) Beneficiary   ( ) Applicant's Account

22. Documents to be presented within _____days after the date of issuance of the shipping document(s) but within validity of the credit.

23. ( ) Please forward the credit to the beneficiary through your correspondents.

24. ( ) Return original credit to this branch for delivery to ourselves.

Guide to the Use of the Form "Application for Documentary Credit"

This guide takes the form of an elaboration of each line of the application form as a means of ready reference. However, it is only a guide and not a technical commentary.

1. Indicate date on which credit will expire, in the country of the beneficiary.

2. The applicant should understand the difference between the three types of credits.

    An **irrevocable credit**, once established, can be cancelled or amended only with the agreement of all parties to the credit.

    A **revocable credit** can be amended or cancelled at anytime without prior warning or notification to the seller (the beneficiary).

    A **transferable credit** can be transferred by the original (first) beneficiary to one or more second beneficiaries subject to certain important conditions.

By airmail/pre-advice by cable/by cable, depending on the urgency of the credit arriving at its destination. A pre-advice is the relay of only brief details. A full cable will include all details and will be the operative instrument; no airmail confirmation will follow.

3. **For Account of** - the full name and address of the applicant for the credit must be shown. The absence of full details will sometimes delay the issuance of the credit.

4. **In Favour of** - the beneficiary's complete name and address must be correctly designated to avoid delays. The use of P.O. boxes to indicate the seller's address should be avoided.

5. **Advising Bank** – Usually the beneficiary's bank or confirming bank where the applicant's bank would send the L/C via swift, tested telex, courier, or air mail.

6. **Currency and Amount** - ensure that the amount will cover the cost of the merchandise plus any other charges which may be permitted to be drawn for. The use of the words "approximately" or "about" allow a tolerance of 10 per cent more or less in the value of the documentary credit.

7. **Partial Shipment** - self explanatory.

   Transhipment - whenever shipments by more than one mode of transport are to be used, such as shipments by both land and sea, transhipments are to be allowed.

8. **Available by** - drafts could be required if drawing is other than sight. Indicate sight or other terms.

9. **For 100% of invoice** - indicate in section 16 if other than 100 per cent.

10. **Shipment/Taking in charge** - to indicate the port or place at which the conveyance of the goods is to commence. Usually port at which vessel is loaded, but may be an inland point at which the terms of delivery indicate shipment will commence.

    No later than - the latest date that goods may be loaded or leave point of shipment.

11. **For Transportation to** - the point at which the buyer is to take charge of the goods.

12. Indicate the number of copies required.

13. Only request this document if you want exporter to complete form. Indicate if more than 5 copies required.

14. & 15.   Indicate if freight paid or payable and if notify party is other than applicant. Freight prepaid or collect must tie in with No. 20 - Terms of delivery.

16. Insurance must at least cover 110 per cent of C.I.F. value of the merchandise.

17. Self explanatory.

18. Indicate in full other documents required.

19. Description of goods should be as precise and concise as possible.

20. **Terms of delivery** - the three most customary terms of delivery are given below:

   (a) (i) **F.O.B. Vessel (Named Port Of Shipment)** - under this term, the seller quotes a price covering all expenses up to and including delivery of goods upon the overseas vessel at the named port of shipment. Insurance is to be covered by the buyer and freight charges will be collected at destination.

   (ii) **F.O.B. Airport** - same as (a)(i), except this term is used when goods are shipped by air and not by sea.

   (b) **C.F.R. (Named Port of Destination)** - under this term, the seller quotes a price including the cost of transportation to the named point of destination. Bills of lading will be marked "freight prepaid." Insurance will be covered by the buyer.

(c) **C.I.F. (Named Port of Destination)** - under this term, the seller quotes a price including the cost of the goods, the marine insurance, and all transportation charges to the named point of destination. Bills of lading will be marked "freight prepaid" and insurance certificate must be presented with the other documents. Such terms as "F.A.S.", ex-store, ex-warehouse, etc., are, in so far as insurance and freight are concerned, similar to F.O.B. Any departure from these basic principles should be explained on the application form.

21. **Special conditions** - specify if other bank charges are to be paid by the buyer or the seller. Other special provisions are to be included in this section.

22. As a general rule, documents should be presented for negotiation as soon as is reasonably possible after shipment has been made so as to allow the relative shipping documents to be in the hands of the consignees before the arrival of the carrying vessel, thereby avoiding demurrage and/or storage charges.

23. & 24.   The applicant's preference for method of delivery of the credit to the beneficiary should be specified here.

UNCONFIRMED AND CONFIRMED LETTERS OF CREDIT

By confirming an irrevocable letter of credit a bank commits itself in the same way as the issuing bank, and in addition to the commitment of the issuing bank.

Quite obviously the nature of that commitment depends upon the type of the credit, which may be any of the following:

- a credit payable at sight;
- a credit payable at a deferred date determined in accordance with the stipulations of the credit;
- a credit payable by acceptance of a tenor draft ; or
- a credit payable by negotiation of a sight draft or of a tenor draft but without recourse to drawers and/or bona fide holders.

It follows that the confirming bank does not automatically undertake to pay the beneficiary immediately upon presentation of conforming documents.

If the credit provides for the drawing of a sight draft on the confirming bank, then that bank must pay at sight when the conforming documents are presented. Similarly, if the credit calls for a tenor draft to be drawn on the confirming bank, then subject to the presentation of conforming documents, that bank should accept the tenor draft payable at a future date and return it to the beneficiary. It might, of course, at the request of the beneficiary and as a separate banking operation, also discount the draft without recourse.

In the case of a deferred payment credit, according to the instructions received, the confirming bank must issue its deferred payment undertaking to the beneficiary, making payment at the prescribed future date.

Where the credit is payable by negotiation, the confirming bank is required to act in accordance with the terms of the above conditions and Article 11(c) of the Uniform Customs and Practice for Documentary Credits (UCPDC 500 - see Chapter 7). It is required to negotiate the draft drawn on the issuing bank or the seller - according to the wording of the credit - to give immediate value minus the interest for the estimated period, before it will receive reimbursement from the issuing bank. However, the negotiation is without recourse in the event of compliant documents.

If a credit calls for a draft, that draft must be drawn at the usance (sight or other) and on the party stipulated in the credit. That party may be, although it is not necessarily, the confirming bank. Parties on which credits may stipulate drafts to be drawn are:

- the advising bank
- the confirming bank
- the issuing bank
- the bank where the credit is available by sight payment or by acceptance
- another party, for example, a reimbursing bank

A bank requested to confirm a credit is never obliged to agree. However if a bank does confirm, it must abide by UCPDC 500. Indeed, banks in North America adhere collectively to this document, and their obligations as confirming banks are those listed in Article 10(b).

By the terms of Article 10(b)(iv), the undertaking of the confirming bank is to negotiate the beneficiary's draft(s) "without recourse to drawers and/or bona fide holders."

The governing proviso is that the stipulated documents must be presented and the credit's terms and conditions complied with. To ascertain whether the proviso has been met, the confirming bank is to examine the documents. When it has and it considers that "they appear on their face to be in accordance with the terms and conditions of the credit," it must negotiate without recourse.

By negotiating without recourse and without using the facility it has under Article 14(f), the confirming bank has accepted in its relationship with the beneficiary that the credit has been properly used. If the documents are then refused by the issuing bank for discrepancies which the confirming bank overlooked, the consequences fall to the account of the confirming bank. It cannot go back to the "drawers and/or bona fide holders" and hold them responsible for its own failure to examine the documents properly.

Confirmation is generally seen as the protection of the beneficiary from both the "country risks" (transfer risks) and the "bank risks" (financial collapse of the issuing bank). Nevertheless, confirmation is not merely based on the risk of country and bank concerned, but, as clearly shown in the wording of Articles 10(b) and 11(d) of UCPDC 500, the confirming bank is responsible for satisfying itself as to the compliant nature of the documents against which it makes payment.

Which Credits Should be Confirmed?

Which credits should be confirmed and why is a debatable question that largely turns on the country risk and the strength of the issuing bank. A downturn in the market may also cause sellers to request confirmation of credits which they normally would not confirm.

When deciding whether or not to confirm a credit these main factors must be examined :

- Credit standing of the issuing bank.
- Economic and political situation in the country where the issuing bank and its parent are located.
- Whether the credit allows T/T reimbursing against a third party bank.
- Currency of a letter of credit (providing high volatility).

Confirmations may not be required where :

- The issuing bank is a first class international bank.
- The issuing bank is located in a country with a stable economy.
- The L/C allows T/T reimbursement against an independent bank.
- The market conditions are stable for the goods covered under the letter of credit.

If the supplier is not confident about any one of these factors, confirming the L/C may make sleeping at night easier.

THE IMPORTANCE OF T/T REIMBURSEMENT IN A LETTER OF CREDIT

It is very important to understand the value of a T/T REIM-BURSEMENT CLAUSE in the letter of credit. The payment clause in a L/C can be worded in many ways, but the essential difference is that a credit can be stipulated to be made payable at the counters of the issuing bank or at the counters of the negotiating bank. A T/T Reimbursement Clause is obviously more beneficial for the seller than the buyer because it gives the seller more security in the L/C negotiation process. Having a properly worded T/T Reimbursement Clause means that as soon as the negotiating bank finds that documents presented under the L/C are in order, it can claim for reimbursement and most likely receive funds three to five days after the claim is sent by tested telex. If the L/C calls for payment at the counters of the issuing bank, then the negotiating bank has to send all documents via courier to the issuing bank and wait until the documents are accepted by the issuing bank prior to receipt of payment. More often than not, a discrepancy will be found in a set of documents presented under a letter of credit. If as in this case, the documents are sent to the counters of the issuing bank for payment and if due to a decline in the market the buyer wants to refuse or delay payment, he has a good chance of success should a spelling mistake or other small discrepancy be found in the documents. Banks have to rely on documents that represent real goods and if the documents have even a minor discrepancy they have to refer back to the applicant (the buyer) for acceptance prior to affecting payment. When a credit specifies T/T reimbursement, the seller is better protected as it is his negotiating bank that will check the documents and then claim reimbursement once all documents are in order as per the L/C terms and conditions. Where a discrepancy is found the negotiating bank will always give the beneficiary a chance to correct the documents presented and resubmit them for negotiation prior to alerting the issuing bank that discrepancies have been found in the documents. This applies when the L/C is issued unconfirmed and the seller has to rely on the strength of the issuing bank and reimbursing bank for payment.

Payment condition allowing T/T Reimbursement can be worded in the following way :

> T/T REIMBURSEMENT ACCEPTABLE. UPON NEGOTIATION, NEGOTIATING BANK IS REQUIRED TO SEND A TESTED TELEX TO THE ISSUING BANK CERTIFYING THAT ALL DOCUMENTS COMPLY WITH L/C TERMS, QUOTING L/C NUMBER, DRAWN AMOUNT, AND INTL. COURIER NUMBER AND DATE. WE SHALL COVER THE NEGOTIATING BANK AS REQUESTED. VALUE 4 WORKING DAYS AFTER DATE OF RECEIPT OF TELEX.

The T/T Reimbursement Clause above looks in order and would be accepted by most beneficiaries of unconfirmed credits. It is interesting to note, however, that the issuing bank wants to make sure that the documents presented under the credit are dispatched to them via courier at the time of the claim. This means that the negotiating bank can only send its tested telex when the documents are put together in a courier pouch and are picked up by the local courier service.

Since most courier companies deliver packages within two to three days there is a good chance that the issuing bank will receive the documents and have a chance to check them before affecting payment under the claim in the four-day required period.

Some "smart" buyers like to open letters of credit with a payment clause that requires the negotiating bank to send documents to their counters for checking, therefore, not allowing T/T reimbursement. The wording of such payment clauses do not explicitly say that a T/T reimbursement is NOT ALLOWED, they just do not say that it is allowed. As the saying goes, "it is sometimes more important what is not said than what is said."

Payment clause NOT allowing T/T Reimbursement could be worded in the following way :

> NEGOTIATE AT SIGHT BASIS AND SEND DOCUMENTS TO US VIA COURIER SERVICE. UPON RECEIPT OF THE DOCUMENTS, WE WILL REMIT FUNDS AS PER YOUR INSTRUCTIONS.

If you are an importer, you want to issue your L/Cs with such a payment clause. You can explain to the beneficiary that your First Class Bank follows the standard practice that all banks follow in checking documents under irrevocable credits according to the UCPDC 500. You can also argue that your bank manager can only allow a letter of credit to be issued with such a payment clause, otherwise, no L/C and no deal.

On the other hand, the beneficiary has the choice of accepting this story or of telling the applicant that unless the L/C is amended, the goods will be sold to another buyer who is willing to accept a T/T Reimbursement Clause in the L/C. If the buyer were then to agree to accept T/T reimbursement, an amendment would have to be made as follows:

> NEGOTIATE AT SIGHT BASIS AND SEEK YOUR REIMBURSEMENT FROM US VIA TESTED TELEX AT LEAST 2 WORKING DAYS BEFORE YOUR VALUE DATE, MENTIONING CLAIM AMOUNT, VALUE DATE, AND SHIPPING DATE, AND STATING THAT ALL TERMS AND CONDITIONS OF CREDIT ARE COMPLIED WITH. UPON RECEIPT OF YOUR CLAIM WE WILL HONOUR IT AS PER YOUR INSTRUCTIONS.

The above two payment clauses are reprinted from an actual L/C transaction where the L/C was first issued not allowing T/T reimbursement and was later amended to allow it.

A trader must always be on the alert when presenting documents in a declining market, under an unconfirmed credit, even with a T/T Reimbursement Clause. If a payment clause states that the reimbursing bank must honour the claim within two working days and does not require the courier number in the telex claim, there is a good chance that the negotiating bank will receive funds under the claim. Where funds are remitted and the issuing bank finds a discrepancy in the documents after it has affected payment, it can still request that the funds be returned and put the documents at the disposal of the beneficiary. In such a case the negotiating bank would debate whether the discrepancy noted by the issuing bank is considered a discrepancy under UCPDC 500 rules and might eventually refer the dispute to the ICC and/or local courts. To help reduce such risks, beneficiaries of letters of credit often choose to add confirmation of their advising bank or a third party bank to the credit.

AUTONOMY OF THE LETTER OF CREDIT AND EXCEPTIONS TO AUTONOMY

A letter of credit is an independent contract that states all of the conditions defining the rights and obligations of the parties. A dispute as to those rights or obligations must be resolved by reference only to the letter of credit and not to any other contract or relationship. The obligation of the issuer to pay must be executed as long as the conditions set out in the credit are met by the beneficiary. This obligation stands irrespective of any dispute between the customer and beneficiary as to partial or full execution of the underlying contract, or of any dispute between the bank and the customer.

The opening of a confirmed letter of credit constitutes a bargain between the banker and the vendor of the goods that imposes on the banker an absolute obligation to pay.

Although the principle of autonomy of the credit is firmly established, the rule is by no means absolute. The risk that an issuing bank undertakes upon its issuance of the credit may be decreased or increased depending on the business imagination and consent of the customer and bank. The issuer may choose to become intimately involved in seeing to the execution of the contract, or retain such an option by so stipulating. Although it is rare to find the issuer of a credit taking more than a documentary and detached involvement in the performance of the underlying contract, it is not uncommon to find reference to performance of the contract in the letter of credit. One is led to query the effect of such wording in the credit upon the principle of autonomy. It may be said that the letter of credit must of necessity make reference to the underlying contract in order to identify the transaction for which documentation and payment under the credit is to relate. However, express and clear wording is required to force the bank to become involved in seeing to the actual performance of the underlying contract.

In a documentary credit, a reference to a contract in the description of goods will only require the beneficiary to reprint the contract number as shown in the L/C description of goods. The bank should not go any further into the contract. Therefore, a letter of credit is an independent contract in itself with regard to payment. With regards to quality claims, provisions for short weight, and other contractual items, the letter of credit stays autonomous and the buyer cannot stop payment unless a court injunction is issued.

Having obtained a basic understanding of what constitutes a sales contract and of how the buyer and seller can come to an agreement of terms through the use of a letter of credit, we can now turn to an examination of the finer points including transferable letters of credit, assignments of proceeds, and back-to-back credits.

Chapter II

THREE WAYS TO MAKE MONEY
WITHOUT MONEY

Excellence is to do a common thing in an uncommon way.
— Booker T. Washington

TRANSFERABLE LETTER OF CREDIT

Article 48 of UCPDC 500 deals with transferable credits (See Chapter 7). In summary it states that the letter of credit

- Is transferable only if expressly designated.
- Is transferred by instruction from the first beneficiary.
- Can be transferred to one or more 'second beneficiaries.'
- Can be transferred only once.
- Must be irrevocable.

What does this mean for you? It means that by using Transferable Credits you can make money without money. You do not need to have a credit line from the bank to transfer a letter of credit (which is deemed transferable) and is issued in your favour. All you have to do is to find a product at a competitive price, and a buyer who is interested in purchasing that product at a higher price. A buyer can be a foreign-based company or a local distributor. Usually trading companies will try to obtain exclusive rights to a product from a specific manufacturer. Having exclusive rights to a product helps the trading company to reduce competition from other traders trying to sell the same item in the same market. However, exclusive rights to a product does not stop other producers of similar products from competing in the same marketplace.

Finding a Product to Trade

A trader always looks for opportunities to trade. These opportunities may take him all over the globe. To illustrate the thinking process a trader might go through prior to choosing a product it is useful to analyse a concrete transaction.

In 1996 building materials were selling well in Russia. One trader, whose country of expertise was Russia, received information from his contacts in Moscow that interior doors were in demand.

After searching through various databases, a Canadian supplier of doors with experience exporting to Russia was found. Having found a supplier, the trader telephoned and introduced himself to the export manager as a trading house based in New York with offices in Moscow, Kiev, and Minsk. The trader told the export manager that he had a request for doors for export and learned during the phone conversation that the supplier had previously exported doors to Russia and Ukraine, but never to Belarus (one of the ex-Soviet Republics now part of the Commonwealth of Independent States). Having contacts in Minsk, the capital city of Belarus, the trader found a focus point, a geographical location where he could market a good quality product that was in demand.

The next thought on the trader's mind was that of exclusive rights. Should he ask the supplier for exclusive rights prior to making the first successful sale or should he first make one good sale and then ask for exclusivity? The trader decided to make a good sale first and then to proceed further with at least one concrete result behind him.

The mathematics of the business transaction were as follows: The cost of an interior hollow door 3.5 x 81 x 200cm ex-works was U.S. $27.35; the primed MDF frame for that door ex-works, U.S. $13.45; thus the total cost for door plus frame ex-works was U.S. $40.80

A forty-foot container of doors and frames that size held about 600 doors. A twenty-foot container shipment was possible but not cost efficient due to the bulk size of the doors and frames.

The cost of transportation of a forty-foot container from the supplier's warehouse in Toronto to the port of Montreal, through a European transhipment port, and then via truck to Minsk, Belarus, was U.S. $5,600/600 = $9.33 (cost of freight per door).

To insure the goods value: [cost ($40.80 per door) + freight ($9.33)] x 600 (doors in forty-foot container) = $30,078 (total value) + 10% = $33,085.80. The insurance cost, 0.8% of invoice value, worked out to $264.69 per container. The insurance policy covered all risk, including war risk, until arrival at the door of the final destination in Minsk.

Having worked out the freight and insurance cost the trader was able to determine the CIP Minsk cost, U.S. $50.57. Now it was time to travel to the local market in Minsk to study the price of importing similar quality doors. Only very rarely do you have a product to which there is no alternative in the market or that is exceptionally superior and deserving of special attention from buyers. However, having a direct source of competitively priced good quality doors and frames gave the trader hope of success.

After arriving in Minsk and talking to importers, wholesalers, and retailers of building materials, the trader learned that a similar doors with frames were being offered for $150 retail and for $100 wholesale. His cost was CIP $50.57. If he could sell each door for $100, the profit of $49.43 per door x 600 doors would result in U.S. $29,658.00 gross profit on a forty-foot container. Sounds too good to be true? Yes.

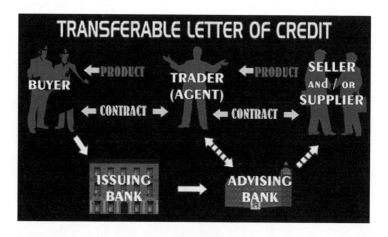

After calculating the import duty and value-added tax, plus other out of pocket expenses, the cost was increased by U.S. $12.00 making the landed cost with duty paid, U.S. $62.57 per door.

The trader found that importers who were able to purchase a container load of doors would pay a maximum of U.S. $75.00 per door duty paid. That meant the gross profit on a forty-foot container of doors would be ($75.00 - $62.57) x 600 or U.S. $7,458.00. After spending two weeks in Minsk, the trader signed contracts for a total of three forty-foot containers, the sales of which would result in a U.S. $22,374.00 gross profit.

In the contract with the importer in Minsk the payment term that was agreed to was an irrevocable, transferable, sight letter of credit issued from a first-class bank, having a T/T reimbursement clause. The trader made sure that the letter of credit did not go into an extensive description of goods. The contract specified the type of door, size, and quantity, but the description of goods in the letter of credit simply read: "Interior doors and frames 600 pcs."

This simple description of goods made the L/C easy to transfer, taking into account that the other documents called for in the L/C consisted of: Commercial Invoice, Packing List, Certificate of Origin, and Full Set of Ocean Bills of Lading. The trader promised to insure the goods at his own expense and negotiated the contracts in such a way that the buyer did not ask for an insurance certificate to be included with the other documents presented under the L/C. If the insurance certificate had been required under the L/C, then the trader would have had difficulty in transferring the credit to the supplier because the difference in the initial (supply) and final (sales) price for the goods meant that an under-valued insurance certificate would have come from the supplier. A solution would have been to purchase another insurance policy for the value in accordance with the original L/C received in the trader's favour, or to ask the supplier to insure the goods for a value greater than actual invoice cost plus 10 per cent.

With bank charges of U.S. $1,000.00 (0.10% of L/C amount) on the transaction of these three containers valued at about U.S. $100,000.00, gross profit amounted to U.S. $21,374.00. Not bad for making money without money.

Many new traders complain that by asking for transferable credits they expose themselves to potential buyers as the middleman rather than as the principal holder of the goods. Often it is difficult to gain the trust and confidence of buyers with whom you do not have personal contacts. Many traders don't know how to resolve this problem, but as you will learn next, Article 49 of UCPDC 500 gives the answer.

Sample Application Form Used by the Royal Bank of Canada to Transfer a Letter of Credit

The Manager
The Royal Bank of Canada
International Trade Centre - Ontario
180 Wellington Street West
Toronto, Ontario M5J 1J1 Canada

Dear Sir:

RE: IRREVOCABLE TRANSFERABLE LETTER OF CREDIT NO.
ISSUED BY :

For value received, the undersigned beneficiary hereby irrevocably transfers to:

all rights of the undersigned beneficiary to draw up to but not exceeding a sum of $_____under the above Letter of Credit, subject to the same terms and conditions with the exception of the following:

Quantity of merchandise: _____
Unit price: _____
Latest shipment date: _____
Expiry date: _____

By this transfer, all rights of the undersigned beneficiary in such Letter of Credit are transferred to the transferee (up to the amount aforesaid) and the transferee shall (up to the amount aforesaid) have the sole rights as beneficiary thereof.

WE IRREVOCABLY AUTHORIZE ROYAL BANK OF CANADA TO TRANSFER ALL THE AMENDMENTS RECEIVED HENCEFORTH TO THE SECOND BENEFICIARY WITHOUT OUR PRIOR CONSENT/ APPROVAL

The undersigned beneficiary agrees to deliver to you on or before the date on which the transferee's draft and documents are presented to you for payment (1) its draft in an amount equal to the difference between the amount of the relative drawing authorized and the amount of the draft drawn by the transferee, so presented; and (2) its commercial invoice(s) to be substituted for the commercial invoice(s) presented to you with the draft drawn by the transferee. In each case, you are requested to deliver to the undersigned beneficiary your check for the amount of the draft of the undersigned beneficiary as described above together with the commercial invoice(s) of the transferee referred to above provided, of course, that you honoured the transferee's draft and also provided that our draft and invoices conform with the conditions of the credit.

Should the undersigned beneficiary fail to deliver to you its draft and commercial invoice(s) as above provided, you are hereby authorized to forward to (or as instructed by) the party on whose request you acted in the letter of credit transaction, the commercial invoice(s) and other relative documents accompanying the draft drawn by the transferee and to use such documents as fully complying with the terms of the letter of credit as then in force. In each such case, you shall have no responsibility to make payment to the undersigned beneficiary of the amount referred to above and you shall have no other responsibility to the undersigned beneficiary.

Kindly notify the transferee in such form as you deem advisable of the terms and conditions of the credit as transferred and after noting the transfer on the original instrument which we are forwarding to you herewith, kindly return it to us together with a copy of your notification to the transferee.

We enclose our cheque for $_____representing your transfer commission and in addition we undertake to pay to you on demand any expenses that may be incurred in connection with this transfer.

Yours very truly,

SIGNATURE/S OF
(Name of Company or Individual)   Name of Beneficiary

AUTHENTICATED BY :   Authorized Signature

Note: A bank is not obliged to transfer a letter of credit to another bank even though the credit is deemed transferable. Usually, though, banks do not deny a client's request to transfer a documentary credit.

ASSIGNMENT OF PROCEEDS

Many traders do not know or do not take full advantage of Article 49 of UCPDC 500 "Assignment of Proceeds."
Article 49 Assignment of Proceeds states that :

THE FACT THAT A CREDIT IS NOT STATED TO BE TRANSFERABLE SHALL NOT AFFECT THE BENEFICIARY'S RIGHT TO ASSIGN ANY PROCEEDS TO WHICH HE MAY BE, OR MAY BECOME, ENTITLED UNDER SUCH CREDIT, IN ACCORDANCE WITH THE PROVISIONS OF THE APPLICABLE LAW. THIS ARTICLE RELATES ONLY TO THE ASSIGNMENT OF PROCEEDS AND NOT TO THE ASSIGNMENT OF THE RIGHT TO PERFORM UNDER THE CREDIT ITSELF."

By being the first beneficiary of a letter of credit, even though the credit is not transferable, you can still assign part or parts of the L/C to one or more beneficiaries. An assignment of proceeds is a much simpler and less expensive than the transfer of a letter of credit (Article 48). It involves only a few paragraphs on a piece of paper signed by the first beneficiary and the banker affecting the assignment. This means that if the first beneficiary presents all the necessary conforming documents under the letter of credit, then the bank undertakes to pay the assignee (second beneficiary) before discounting the balance of the L/C to the first beneficiary. It is the first beneficiary's responsibility to prepare all documents for the bank, put together bills of lading, invoices, certificates of origin, and insurance certificates if need be. If there is a discrepancy in the documents and the negotiating bank rejects the documents then the second beneficiary or assignee logically will not get paid until the documents are presented in conformity to the L/C or the applicant accepts discrepant documents and authorizes the issuing bank to pay. The assignee must trust that the assignor will be able to present all documents required by the L/C accurately and on time. If the assignor fails in this task and the letter of credit expires, the assignee is at risk. With a transferable letter of credit, if the second beneficiary has control over the negotiable documents, it is that beneficiary's responsibility to present all documents required by the transferable L/C to his or her bank. Under the assignment of proceeds, however, the beneficiary of the assignment must hand all documents directly to the first beneficiary of the L/C. The assignee has no obligation and no liability under the original credit. All he/she has is a piece of paper issued by the negotiating bank declaring that it will pay the assignee as instructed, when funds are received from the issuing bank, or within a certain time (2 - 3 working days) upon finding the documents in order in the case of a confirmed L/C.

For trading companies, an assignment of proceeds is a very inexpensive and convenient way to do business. It is much more efficient than a transferable letter of credit. Unfortunately, many manufacturers have difficulty understanding the concept of the assignment of proceeds and, even if they understand the theory, they have a hard time trusting that the trading company will present all documents to the bank in proper order. The manufacturer must take the risk of releasing production based on an assignment of proceeds. As the assignee, the manufacturer's worry is, what happens if something goes wrong? Answering this question requires looking at the documents required under a particular L/C and determining who will be responsible for the drafting and presentation of these documents. If a letter of credit can be simply negotiated against standard shipping documents, including an invoice, bills of lading, certificate of origin, and a packing list, there is a good chance that the transaction will be completed, providing that the goods are shipped on or before the latest shipment date and documents are presented to the bank prior to L/C expiry.

The risk can be evaluated by noting which documents are issued outside the beneficiary's control. In this latter case, the Bill of Lading is the only such document. A convincing case can therefore be made to the manufacturer that the assignment will proceed without problems.

If the trading company can convince the manufacturer that it is capable of obtaining all documents required for L/C negotiation on time, and then can present them to the bank holding the original L/C and pay the manufacturers under the assignment seven to ten days after the documents are presented, the trading company has found a way to make money without money, through the use of assignment of proceeds. A trading company can create sales of any product in any country without investing its own capital in inventory, labour, or warehousing costs.

The most difficult challenge is to receive a workable L/C with realistic terms that can be met by all parties involved (in other words, documents can be presented to the bank in due time and goods shipped prior to latest shipment date).

Once a workable L/C is received, even though it may not be transferable, you must remember that you can still assign proceeds to your supplier(s). A trader can educate manufacturers to accept business based on an assignment of proceeds rather than transferable credits. Once the goods have been shipped the trader would obtain the bills of lading from the shipping company, put them together with the invoice, pricing list, certificate of origin, insurance, along with any other documents, and send them to the bank. The bank would then pay the producer the portion assigned from the buyer's L/C, usually the greater part. The difference left over is the trader's profit.

An assignment of proceeds can also be used to pay for freight charges. These charges can amount to U.S. $350,000.00 or more per vessel. Having six or seven shipments per month totalling millions of dollars, the assignment of proceeds can help a company improve cash flow. With an assignment in hand, the ship owner would make sure that the bills of lading are issued in strict compliance with the letter of credit. As the correctness of documents under the L/C has direct bearing on the successful negotiation of the credit, the assignee, in this case the ship owner, is directly interested in swift presentation of conforming documents to the bank.

Usually, agents who represent vessel owners or vessel owners themselves insist on full payment for freight prior to releasing the original bills of lading. Accepting an assignment of proceeds would mean that payment would most probably be received within two weeks from the date of release of original bills of lading to the assignor. These two weeks represent the approximate time necessary to prepare other documents required under a letter of credit and the time the bank needs to check the documents and affect payment.

A trader can explain to the vessel owner that having control of the cargo, which in most cases is worth much more than the cost of freight, gives the vessel owner full security of payment. The rest is a process of negotiation.

The assignment of proceeds presents many advantages to the trader, "the Assignor." Nonetheless, it does present more risk to the supplier, "the Assignee," than a transferable of letter of credit. There are ways, however, to limit the risk of non-performance by the trader assigning proceeds of a letter of credit received in his company's favour.

ASSIGNMENT OF PROCEEDS

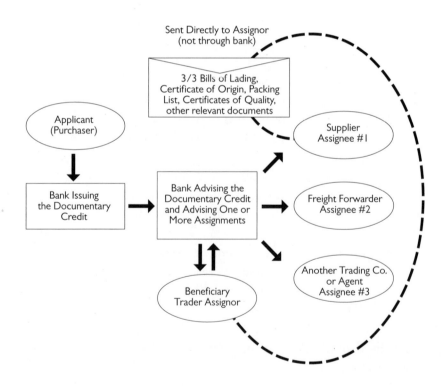

Sample Application to Assign Proceeds of a Letter of Credit Used by the Royal Bank of Canada

TO: ROYAL BANK OF CANADA
INTERNATIONAL TRADE CENTRE - ONTARIO
180 WELLINGTON ST., W., 9TH FLOOR
TORONTO, ONTARIO M5J 1J1

Gentlemen:

Re: Letter of Credit No.

Issued by:

Expiring: _____ Your ref. no.: _____

We hereby authorise and direct you to pay the proceeds of each draft drawn by us, payable to your order, under and in compliance with the above described Letter of Credit (herein called the "Credit"), if and when such draft is honoured, an amount or amounts not exceeding in the aggregate CAD/USD _____

To:_____ whose address is_____
(herein called the Designated Payee"), and to pay the balance, if any, of such proceeds to us.

This instrument, and your acceptance thereof, is not a transfer or assignment of the Credit, does not give to the Designated Payee any interest therein and does not affect our or your right to agree to amendments thereto, the cancellation thereof, or any substitution therefor.

We warrant to you that we have not and will not, by negotiation of drafts or otherwise, transfer or assign the right to receive the whole or any part of such proceeds, and that we have not and will not give any other authorization or direction to make any payment of such proceeds to any third party.

Please advise the Designated Payee of your acceptance of this instrument and, in consideration thereof, we agree that this instrument is irrevocable.

We transmit to you herewith the original Credit including all amendments (if any) and request you to note thereon the foregoing authorization and direction, and also enclose our cheque for CAD/USD _____ to cover your charges.

Yours very truly,

SIGNATURE AND AUTHORITY
TO SIGN GUARANTEED.

NAME AND ADDRESS OF BANK   NAME OF BENEFICIARY

AUTHORIZED SIGNATURE   AUTHORIZED SIGNATURE(S)

We accept the foregoing instrument.

How Can a Supplier Receive an Assignment of Proceeds in His Favour and Limit the Risk of Non-Performance by The Assignor?

Having been on both sides of the trade, I have issued assignments of proceeds and received assignments of proceeds in my favour. Knowing the risks associated with the potential inability of the assignor to put all documents in order under a letter of credit, I have developed a system that allows the assignee to control all the documents needed for successful L/C negotiation. The best way to explain this system is to analyse a particular transaction involving an assignment of proceeds among the following players: 1) the End buyer, L/C applicant "Indian Pipe Distributor"(IPD), 2) the Beneficiary/Assignor "Trading Company"(TC) and, 3)and the Supplier/Assignee: "Another Trading Company"(ATC).

A trading company (TC), having a close relationship with an Indian Pipe Distributor (IPD), contracts to purchase pipes from another trading company (ATC) which is acting as a principal in the transaction. The TC in the purchase contract with ATC negotiates an assignment of proceeds as payment mechanism for the pipes. The TC wants to avoid at all costs disclosing to its buyer, IPD, the fact that it is purchasing these pipes from another trading company and not from a producer directly. The TC could potentially ask its banker to do a back-to-back credit, but some parts of the original credit are structured such that a back-to-back transaction is difficult to execute and TC does not want to put up the cash collateral requested by the negotiating bank for such a transaction. ATC understands the risks associated with an assignment of proceeds, but because the contract is signed on a CFR basis, ATC is in full control of the original Bills of Lading and the only documents it cannot control are the first beneficiary's drafts and invoices. A solution is found by having the advising/negotiating bank, in this case the Hongkong Bank of Canada, HOLD blank letterheads and bills of exchange pre-signed by the assignor at its counters. Having received these pre-signed documents from the beneficiary of the L/C (assignor), Hongkong Bank of Canada could then undertake in its assignment of proceeds to ATC (assignee) that in the event that the assignor were to fail to submit the necessary documents within the time limit provided by the credit, the bank could and would authorise the assignee to use these blank and pre-signed forms to complete any invoices, packing lists, weight lists, beneficiary's certificates, drafts, or other documents required under the L/C. Of course this would only be done if something were to happen to the assignor which interfered with its ability to fulfil the obligations it normally would under a letter of credit. In most cases, the assignor is highly motivated to receive the necessary documents from the assignee as soon as possible in order to negotiate the L/C.

The ATC was meticulous in one other important point which further strengthened its position as the assignee or "second beneficiary" of the L/C. It requested the advising/negotiating bank to certify in the text of the assignment that any amendments to the L/C would have to be approved by the assignee prior to acceptance by the TC assignor.

It goes without saying that in general the assignee would receive a copy of the original L/C from the TC assignor prior to accepting an assignment of proceeds. Having examined all terms and conditions of the export L/C except the price of goods (blanked out by the beneficiary/assignor), the assignee could determine if it could comply, knowing that no amendments could be made without its approval. In essence ATC now had in hand an indirect payment instrument that had a similar function as a documentary letter of credit. Regarding the strength of the issuing bank and whether or not the original L/C was confirmed, in this transaction the L/C was issued by the State Bank of India and was confirmed by Hongkong Bank of Canada. The TC was initially against confirming the L/C as it believed that there was no need because of both the strength of the State Bank of India and its location in a country with relatively low risk at the time. The assignee, however, insisted on having the L/C confirmed by the Hongkong Bank of Canada in order to be certain that once the documents were found to be in conformity to the L/C by the confirming bank, the funds would be paid under the assignment at sight.

A copy of the actual assignment of proceeds covering this transaction is reprinted below. Some information is deleted for reasons of confidentiality.

Example: Assignment of Proceeds (Documentary Credit)

TO: HONGKONG BANK OF CANADA   DATE:
                                     YOUR REF:

Dear Sirs:

Re: Issuing Bank: State Bank of India
Documentary Credit No. :   62437789

We, the undersigned, as beneficiary, hereby assign, authorize, and direct you to remit the proceeds of our drawing(s) under and in compliance with the above described Documentary Credit (hereinafter referred to as the ("Credit") to the Assignee, as follows:

1. To: ATC
Address:
(herein referred to as the ("Assignee") in accordance with the following applicable subdivision which we have completed:

    (a) The sum of $ 750,000.00 in the aggregate;

    (b) — % of the amount of each drawing but not exceeding
      $ — in aggregate;

    (c) At the rate of $ 750.00 per MT (unit(s), weight, measure, or number of) not exceeding $ 825,000.00 in aggregate;

    (d) Not to exceed $ 825,000.00.

In the event this Assignment does not apply to the full proceeds of the credit, pay any balance to us.

2. Please advise the Assignee of your acceptance of the Assignment, and in consideration thereof, we agree that this Assignment is irrevocable and cannot be cancelled or amended without the agreement of the Assignee.

3. We transmit to you herewith the original Credit (including all amendments, if any) and request you to endorse thereon the foregoing Assignment.

To cover your commissions, we authorize you to debit our account No. 400 - 1780 with your Branch No.423. We further agree to pay to you on demand any expenses which may be incurred by you in connection with this Assignment instruction.

4. Additional applicable terms and provisions:

    (a) This assignment, and your acceptance thereof, is not a transfer or assignment of the Credit, and does not give to the Assignee any interest therein. We hereby agree that we will not solely accept any amendments to this Documentary Credit without the consent of the Assignee and we further undertake to provide you with the Assignee's agreement to any amendment prior to our acceptance of the amendment.

    (b) We also enclose together with this assignment, 20 blank and pre-signed letterheads and 20 blank and pre-signed bills of exchange.

In the event that we failed to submit the necessary documents within 15 days from date of Bills of Lading (which will be presented by Assignee directly to you together with other applicable documents) covering shipment of goods called for under the above Credit, we hereby authorize you to use these blank and pre-signed forms to complete any invoices, packing lists, weight lists, beneficiary's certificate, and/or other documents for negotiation under the Credit, and if necessary obtain approval from the issuing bank in respect of discrepancies in the documents.

In case of a term credit, upon your acceptance of documents in full compliance with the terms and conditions of the Credit, and subject to your acceptance of the bank and country risks of the Issuing Bank at the time of negotiation, please discount the bill and pay the Assignee at sight basis, as specified under clause 1 above, under our full risks and responsibilities.

We agree to be charged with interest for the period between the date of your payment to the Assignee until the date of payment by the Issuing Bank, and with any charges incurred by you or your correspondents in connection with this Credit.

(c) We warrant to you that other than as set forth above, we have not and will not by transfer or assignment of the Credit or by negotiation of drafts or otherwise, assign the right to receive the whole or any part of the above proceeds of the Credit or give any other authorization or direction to make any payment thereof to any other party.

(d) This Assignment is valid until the current expiration date of the Credit or any extension of such expiration date for any payment(s) effected under the Credit, as the Credit may from time to time be amended.

(e) In the event of any refusal by you to make payment upon any draft drawn under the Credit, the Assignee will not have any rights against you and shall be bound by your determination. We agree forthwith to return to you any funds inadvertently paid to us.

We further agree to indemnify you for and hold you harmless from and against any cost, liability, or expense, including reasonable attorney's fees to which you may become subject, direct or indirectly, in connection with this assignment.

Yours very truly,
Signature Guaranteed

Assignor

Name of Beneficiary   Name of Bank

Authorized Signature   Authorized Signature

Please print or type Signor's   Please print or type Signor's
Name and Title   Name and Title

DO NOT DETACH

To: ATC (Assignee)
    Full address

Date: Our ref:

Dear Sirs:

Please be advised that we are holding on file the original of this instrument showing yourselves as designated assignee in part 1 and we have accepted the instructions contained therein.

Yours very truly,
HONGKONG BANK OF CANADA

Authorized Signature

BACK-TO-BACK LETTER OF CREDIT

A back-to-back letter of credit consist of two entirely separate documentary credits, but one credit may act as security for the other. They apply in transactions when original suppliers and ultimate buyers deal through a trader. Back-to-back credits are in fact used in the same way as transferable credits, but the rights and obligations of the parties differ in each type of credit.

If the supplier insists on a documentary credit, the trader may apply to his bankers and have them issue one on his behalf. If the trader's bankers are satisfied as to his creditworthiness, they will issue the credit in the normal way and no other formalities will apply. However, the 'back-to-back' aspect comes into play if the trader's bankers insist that the trader obtain a documentary credit in his favour from the ultimate buyer as security for the one which the trader has applied for in favour of the seller.

Only the trader and his banker know of the back-to-back arrangement. The ultimate buyer, the original supplier, and their bankers, are not affected in any way whatsoever by this situation.

Procedure for Arranging Back-to-Back Credits

(1) The trader asks the ultimate buyer to arrange a documentary credit in his favour. This is known as the 'first credit' or 'prime credit.'

(2) The trader then requests his banker to issue a credit in favour of the supplier of the goods. This is known as the 'second credit' or 'issued credit' and the trader is the applicant for the second credit. The second credit will not be issued until the first one has been advised.

(3) The second credit must call for the same documents as the first credit, apart from the invoices, and must have an earlier expiry date and be for a lower amount than the first credit.

Execution of Back-to-Back Credit

(1) The documents are presented via the supplier's advising bank to the issuing bank, which is the bank of the trader. This issuing bank pays the supplier, debiting the trader by way of a separate loan.

(2) The trader's bank then substitutes the supplier's invoices for those of the trader. The bill of exchange will be for a higher amount and will agree with the amount on the new invoice.

(3) The trader's bank, as advising bank of the first credit, presents the documents to the issuing bank.

(4) The issuing bank of the first credit pays in accordance with the terms, debiting the cost to the ultimate buyer.

(5) On receipt of the proceeds of the first credit, the trader's bank clears the loan account in the name of the trader and any surplus represents the trader's profit.

Risks and Liabilities of Back-to-Back Credit

The second credit is an entirely separate instrument, and thus the trader and his bank are responsible for paying the second credit irrespective of whether payment is subsequently received under the first credit.

The second credit must have an earlier expiry date than the first, otherwise the documents required to procure payment under the first credit would not be available in time. It is a good precaution to make the second credit expire in the place of issue otherwise the issuing bank is in the hands of the postal authorities, and delayed receipt of documents could mean non-payment under the first credit. The supplier may insist, however, in having the L/C expiry at his bank's counters, in his country, either because he wants to discount the credit or for other reasons. This problem can be solved by increasing the time allowed to present documents under the first credit and shortening the time given to supplier to present documents under the second credit. It is good practice for both credits to make allowance for third party documents in light of the fact that documents would be presented from various sources.

Difference between Transferable and Back to Back Credits

With transferable credits the ultimate buyer may be aware that he is dealing with a trader (not with a supplier directly); with back-to-back credits he is not. With transferable credits the trader and his bankers have no liability, but with back-to-back credits they are fully liable on the second credit.

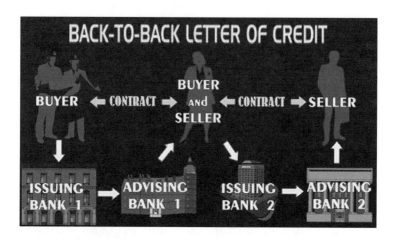

Insurance in Back-to-Back Credits

Where the Second Credit Does Not Call for an Insurance Document: In this case the trader's bankers must make sure that their customer has insured and can produce the appropriate document in time for presentation under the first credit.

Where the Second Credit Calls for an Insurance Document: Care must be taken to stipulate that the amount of insurance evidenced in the document required by the second credit is sufficient to meet the amount of insurance required by the first credit.

Back-to-Back Credit vs. Front-to-Back Credits

Unless you are a well-established trader, banks in North America may avoid taking the risk of back-to-back credits, and even major European trade finance banks who are accustomed to back-to-back business may not want to take the liability. You will need to establish a line of credit for back-to-back business and may even be required to put up some cash collateral. It is therefore advisable when starting in the international trade business to utilize transferable letters of credit and assignments of proceeds. If asking for transferable credits exposes you to your buyers as a trader, it is best to admit that you are, but you should also explain that you have a special and perhaps "exclusive" relationship with the supplier and that you prefer to use the instrument of a transferable credit for payment. If you cannot disclose to these buyers that you are not the ultimate source, then you must educate the supplier to accept an assignment of proceeds instead of a letter of credit or a transfer of a letter of credit. If the supplier agrees, then your buyer will issue a simple irrevocable L/C in your favour and you will in turn assign proceeds to the supplier and where necessary, as in a CFR or CIF sale, for the freight charge. Once you have established yourself in the trading business, the banks may allow you to issue front-to-back letters of credit using perhaps 10 per cent of the L/C value as collateral. Front-to-back means that your bank can issue a letter of credit to a supplier before receiving a letter of credit from your buyer (the first credit).

A front-to-back situation allows a trader great financing ability and purchasing power. Essentially a trader can use the bank's finances to purchase goods all over the world, take positions on commodities, and bid on projects. If a trader is confident that he/she will receive that first L/C, then, the ability to issue a front-to-back credits may be a great asset. However, the risk associated with exposing oneself to a purchase while not having a payment instrument for the sale in place is equally great - even when selling to large respectable corporations. It is not advisable to commit to a purchase prior to receiving a workable L/C. Experience demonstrates that most of the time a documentary credit will require amendments. If the amendments are minor, you might occasionally accept or take a calculated risk; however, if the L/C is considered non-workable unless amendments are done, then you must chase the buyer for such amendments prior to committing yourself to the purchase.

With a front-to-back credit you are committed and are liable to take delivery of the goods. In a situation structured exactly back-to-back, you as the trader are protected because your commitments to the supplier are a mirror of the buyer's commitment to you.

Example: Back-to-Back Credit Purchase of Steel in China and Sale to Spain: The Prime Credit

ISSUED TO A TRADING COMPANY, "STEEL TRADER INTERNA-
TIONAL," ACTING AS A PRINCIPAL IN THE TRANSACTION, BY
A EUROPEAN STEEL MILL (BUYER)

DATE OF ISSUE: 06-Nov-97: 16:52

To: Negotiating Bank, address ...

From: Issuing Bank, address ...

Date: 06.November.1997

TEST   FOR USD   1,970,000.00

:15 TEST KEY: 457587

ON USD 1,970,000.00

WE HAVE ISSUED THE UNDERMENTIONED DOCUMENTARY
CREDIT WHICH IS SUBJECT TO THE U.C.P.D.C. AS PER PUBLICA-
TION NO. 500 OF THE I.C.C. REVISION 1993.

IRREVOCABLE DOCUMENTARY CREDIT 02579860

DATE OF ISSUE: 06.NOVEMBER. 1997
DATE AND PLACE OF EXPIRY: 21.FEBRUARY.1998
IN LONDON

APPLICANT: "EUROPEAN STEEL MILL" (FULL ADDRESS)

BENEFICIARY: STEEL TRADER INTERNATIONAL (FULL ADDRESS)

AVAILABLE WITH:
ADVISING BANK AGAINST PRESENTATION OF THE DOCU-
MENTS DETAILED HEREIN.

AMOUNT: USD 1,970,000

SPECIFIED AS FOLLOWS: 10 PER CENT MORE OR 10 PER CENT LESS ALLOWED

SHIPMENT/DISPATCH FROM: SHANGHAI/CHINA
TRANSPORTATION TO: BILBAO/SPAIN
SHIPMENT LATEST: 31.JANUARY.1998

PERIOD FOR PRESENTATION:
DOCUMENTS TO BE PRESENTED WITHIN 21 DAYS AFTER THE DATE OF ISSUANCE OF THE TRANSPORT DOCUMENT(S).

CHARGES
ALL BANK CHARGES OUTSIDE THE ISSUING BANK'S COUNTRY ARE FOR BENEFICIARY'S ACCOUNT.

SHIPMENT (OF GOODS)
HOT ROLLED STEEL PLATES AS PER CONTRACT NO. 97102607.P1

QUANTITY: 5000 MT

TOLERANCE IN QUANTITY: 10 PER CENT MORE OR LESS.
MARKINGS: EACH PLATE HAS TO BE STAMPED WITH HEAT NUMBER, DIMENSION.

PRICE: USD 394,00 PER MT EFFECTIVE, CFR FO CQD BILBAO, SPAIN.

DOCUMENTS REQUIRED:
1. SIGNED COMMERCIAL INVOICE IN TRIPLICATE, SHOWING MATERIAL DESCRIPTION AS PER L/C, NUMBER OF PIECES, AND WEIGHT PER DIMENSION.

2. OCEAN BILL OF LADING, 3/3 ORIGINAL AND 3 NON-NEGOTIABLE, MADE OUT TO ORDER, BLANK ENDORSED, MARKED: CLEAN ON BOARD, SHIPPED UNDER DECK, FREIGHT PREPAID AS PER CHARTER PARTY. SHOWING CARRIER WITH FULL NAME AND ADDRESS, SHIPPING MARKS, NUMBER OF PLATES, AND WEIGHT FOR EACH DIMENSION SEPARATELY. MATERIAL DESCRIPTION: HOT

ROLLED STEEL PLATES, EVIDENCING SHIPMENT FROM SHANGHAI/ CHINA TO BILBAO, SPAIN, STAMPED AND SIGNED BY MASTER OF CARRYING VESSEL. CHARTER PARTY AND B/L CLAUSED ATMOSPHERICAL RUST DUE TO UNPRO-TECTED STORAGE IN OPEN AREA ARE ACCEPTABLE.

3. CERTIFICATE OF ORIGIN ISSUED BY CHAMBER OF COM-MERCE OF P.R.C., CHINA.

4. BENEFICIARY'S CONFIRMATION THAT MILL TEST CERTIFI-CATES WITH CHEMICAL AND MECHANICAL VALUES FOR EACH MELT ISSUED BY PRODUCING MILL, ISSUED TO WHOM IT MAY CONCERN. APPROVAL STAMPING AND SIGNATURE SHOWING MATERIAL DESCRIPTION AS PER L/C, NO. OF PIECES, DIMENSION, AND WEIGHT, EACH CERTIFICATE REQUIRED IN DUPLICATE, PACKING LIST AS WELL AS ONE SET OF NON-NEGOTIABLE DOCUMENTS HAVE BEEN SENT DIRECTLY TO THE BUYER WITHIN 8 DAYS.

5. DECLARATION OF BENEFICIARY CERTIFYING: THAT SHIP-MENT WILL BE EFFECTED BY VESSEL NOT OLDER THAN 15 YEARS.

INSTRUCTION TO THE CORRESPONDENT:
UPON RECEIPT BY US OF YOUR DULY TESTED TELEX, CERTIFY-ING PAYMENT AND DESPATCH IMMEDIATELY TO US OF CREDIT COMPLYING DOCUMENTS BY DHL COURIER SERVICE (MEN-TIONING PICK-UP DATE AND AIRWAY BILL NO.) WE SHALL COVER YOU AS PER YOUR INSTRUCTIONS AT MATURITY. DOCUMENTS TO BE SENT TO ISSUING BANK, FULL ADDRESS.

CONFIRMATION INSTRUCTIONS:
WE REQUEST YOU TO NOTIFY THE BENEFICIARY WITHOUT ADDING YOUR CONFIRMATION.

PRESENT TELEX CONTAINS ALL DETAILS OF THE CREDIT AND IS TO BE CONSIDERED AS THE OPERATIVE INSTRUMENT.

PLEASE ACKNOWLEDGE RECEIPT.

Steel slab produced by Azovstal Iron and Steel Works Ukraine being unloaded in the port of Shanghai (Photo by Author).

Steel plate produced by Shanghai No.3 Iron and Steels Works from the Ukrainian slab shown above ready for export to Europe.

Second Letter of Credit (Issued Credit) "The Back Credit"

ISSUED TO CHINA STEEL PRODUCER (SUPPLIER) BY "STEEL TRADER INTERNATIONAL" (FOR RE-SALE TO EUROPEAN STEEL MILL)

ADDRESS: BANK OF CHINA
FROM: NEGOTIATING BANK , LONDON
DATE: 10 NOVEMBER 1997
TEST ON USD 1,895,000 - DTD 10.NOV.97

ATTN LC DEPT:
PLEASE ADVISE CHINA STEEL PRODUCER THAT WE ISSUE IN THEIR FAVOUR OUR IRREVOCABLE DOCUMENTARY CREDIT NUMBER BACK 21165 DETAILED AS FOLLOWS:

APPLICANT: "STEEL TRADER INTERNATIONAL"
               (FULL ADDRESS)
BENEFICIARY: CHINA STEEL PRODUCER (FULL ADDRESS)
L/C AMOUNT: USD 1,895,000.00 +/-10 PCT
               SAY ONE MILLION EIGHT HUNDRED AND NINETY-FIVE THOUSAND US DOLLARS PLUS OR MINUS TEN PER CENT
EXPIRY DATE: 14TH JANUARY 1998 IN LONDON

THIS LETTER OF CREDIT IS AVAILABLE WITH NEGOTIATING BANK, LONDON (STEEL TRADER'S BANK) FOR PAYMENT AT SIGHT AGAINST PRESENTATION OF THE FOLLOWING DOCUMENTS:

DOCUMENTS REQUIRED:
1. SIGNED COMMERCIAL INVOICE IN TRIPLICATE, SHOWING MATERIAL DESCRIPTION AS PER L/C, NUMBER OF PIECES, AND WEIGHT PER DIMENSION.

2. OCEAN BILL OF LADING, 3/3 ORIGINAL AND 3 NON-NEGOTIABLE, MADE OUT TO ORDER, BLANK ENDORSED, MARKED: CLEAN ON BOARD, SHIPPED UNDER DECK, FREIGHT PREPARED AS PER CHARTER   PARTY. SHOWING CARRIER WITH FULL NAME AND ADDRESS, SHIPPING MARKS, NUMBER OF PLATES, AND WEIGHT FOR EACH DIMENSION SEPARATELY. MATERIAL DESCRIPTION: PRIME

HOT ROLLED STEEL PLATES, EVIDENCING SHIPMENT FROM SHANGHAI, CHINA TO BILBAO, SPAIN STAMPED AND SIGNED BY MASTER OF CARRYING VESSEL. CHARTER PARTY, AND B/L CLAUSED 'ATMOSPHERICAL RUST DUE TO UNPRO-TECTED STORAGE IN OPEN AREA' ARE ACCEPTABLE.

3. CERTIFICATE OF ORIGIN ISSUED BY CHAMBER OF COM-MERCE OF P.R.C., CHINA.

4. BENEFICIARY'S CERTIFICATE CONFIRMING THAT ONE SET OF NON-NEGOTIABLE DOCUMENTS AND MILL TEST CER-TIFICATES HAVE BEEN SENT DIRECTLY TO BENEFICIARY WITHIN 3 DAYS AFTER BILL OF LADING. ORIGINAL COU-RIER RECEIPT IS REQUIRED FOR NEGOTIA TION.

5. PACKING AND WEIGHT LIST IN TRIPLICATE.

6. CERTIFICATE OF QUALITY AND QUANTITY, ISSUED BY C.C.I.B. IN TRIPLICATE.

7. ORIGINAL FORM-A DOCUMENT FOR DESTINATION SPAIN.

8. MILL TEST CERTIFICATES ISSUED 'TO WHOM IT MAY CON-CERN' WITH APPROVAL STAMPING AND SIGNATURE SHOWING MATERIAL DESCRIPTION AS PER L/C, NO. OF PIECES, DIMENSION, AND WEIGHT, SHOWING THE ME-CHANICAL PROPERTIES REQUIRED IN DUPLICATE.

9. BENEFICIARY'S DECLARATION THAT SHIPMENT WAS EF-FECTED BY VESSEL NOT OLDER THAN 15 YEARS.

COVERING SHIPMENT (OF GOODS)
HOT ROLLED STEEL PLATES AS PER CONTRACT NO. 97102607.P1.

QUANTITY: 5000 MT

TOLERANCE ON QUANTITY: 10 PER CENT MORE OR LESS. MARKINGS: EACH PLATE HAS TO BE STAMPED WITH HEAT NUMBER, DIMENSION.

PRICE: USD 379.00 PER MT EFFECTIVE, CFR FO CQD BILBAO,
         SPAIN

SHIPMENT/DISPATCH FROM: SHANGHAI/CHINA
TRANSPORTATION TO: BILBAO/SPAIN
SHIPMENT LATEST: 31 DECEMBER 1997
PARTIAL SHIPMENT: PROHIBITED
TRANSHIPMENT: PROHIBITED

SPECIAL INSTRUCTIONS:
1. DOCUMENTS TO BE PRESENTED WITHIN 14 DAYS AFTER
   THE DATE   OF ISSUANCE OF THE TRANSPORT
   DOCUMENT(S) BUT WITHIN THE VALIDITY OF THE L/C
   VALIDITY.

2. ALL BANK CHARGES OTHER THAN ISSUING BANK'S ARE
   FOR BENEFICIARY'S ACCOUNT.

3. DOCUMENTS TO BE REMITTED IN ONE LOT BY COURIER
   DIRECTLY   TO: NEGOTIATING BANK (TRADER'S BANK)
   (FULL ADDRESS)

4. NO DOCUMENTS OTHER THAN COMMERCIAL INVOICE TO
   STATE VALUE OF GOODS, SHIPMENT TERMS OR THIS
   LETTER OF CREDIT NUMBER.

UPON RECEIPT BY US OF CREDIT COMPLYING DOCUMENTS
WE UNDERTAKE TO REMIT FUNDS AS PER YOUR INSTRUC-
TIONS.

THIS TELEX IS THE OPERATIVE INSTRUMENT AND NO MAIL
CONFIRMATION WILL FOLLOW.

ISSUED SUBJECT TO THE UNIFORM CUSTOMS AND PRACTICE
FOR DOCUMENTARY CREDITS (1993 REVISION) ICC PUBLICA-
TION NO. 500.

REGARDS,
L/C DEPT.

The gross profit on this transaction before L/C charges is U.S. $75,000. The cost to issue a back-to-back credit from a West European bank is about 0.25-0.40 per cent per quarter calculated on the L/C amount. Considering the value of the second credit, U.S. $1,895,000, and the fact that the sight transaction would not extend beyond three months, the bank charges would equal about U.S. $4,737-$7,580. Not withstanding other expenses STEEL TRADER INTERNATIONAL made U.S. $70,263-$67,420 on this back-to-back transaction without investing a penny in inventory, using the buyer's money to make money.

CHOOSING THE BEST STRUCTURE

Once you have learned how to transfer letters of credit, assign proceeds, and structure back-to-back letters of credit, you have learned the art of making money without money. You must choose the best structure for yourself when negotiating a specific trade deal. It is advisable to treat each deal independently from previous transactions and depending on the circumstances, decide whether a transfer, assignment, or back-to-back is more appropriate.

By accepting a first letter of credit in your company's favour, your company becomes a principal in a transaction. Even when you transfer the credit to a second beneficiary you still control the deal as the second beneficiary has to present invoices in your company's name. You then substitute these invoices and other applicable documents for your own documents and negotiate the credit.

Assignment of proceeds is a good payment instrument because it is the simplest and least expensive to implement. Most important, if you are just starting in the international trade business, you can accept letters of credit which are not transferable, and still be able to assign proceeds and appear to be an independent principal in the transaction. If you are able to convince the supplier to accept an assignment of proceeds as method of payment you are halfway there. For the other half, you must gain the trust of the buyer such that he will issue a workable L/C in your company's favour. Buyers may sometimes affect credit checks on your company prior to issuing such a letter of credit. If your company has no credit history it may help to get a letter of recommendation from a banker who can attest to your good name. Buyers will sometimes also request that a performance bond be issued as security, usually for 2 per cent of the contract value, to be drawn in case of non-performance. If the contract is worth millions of dollars, a trader may not have the funds needed to establish a performance bond as the bank issuing it would probably require 100 per cent cash collateral. One solution would be to offer the buyer better contract terms and therefore provide incentives for the buyer not to require a performance bond. Changing terms of sale from FOB to CFR or CIF may help to convince the buyer that a performance bond is not necessary. That you will be chartering the vessel or ordering the container and purchasing insurance at your own expense demonstrates an undertaking of performance.

Back-to-back credits are more difficult to arrange, may require partial security to be established, and are usually more costly than assignments. Some banks, however, may charge the same issuing cost for a back-to-back or a transfer of credit because both require detailed analysis and matching of documents.

A transfer of a letter of credit does not require that the beneficiary provide any collateral. However, the second beneficiary, the supplier, knows that you have transferred someone else's L/C. It is not a crime to transfer a letter of credit, but it may be good for business to inform the buyer from the start that yes, you are a trader who is putting the deal together.

The relationship you as a trader have with a supplier may be more important than your relationship with a particular buyer. If you can develop an exclusivity for goods that are in demand on the market, you can set the rules of the trade. If the source of supply is scarce or competitive in the market, buyers will accept any payment terms you set, as long as the product is delivered on time and at the right price.

The role of trading houses and agents who work for commissions from either the buyer's or seller's side is very important in the market. Traders are the driving force in global trade. It is the trader who spends sleepless nights making long distance calls or sending fax or e-mail messages to ensure that a particular deal will take place. Many suppliers will confirm that their export business depends on local traders who promote their products.

Chapter III

STANDBY LETTERS OF CREDIT AND PERFORMANCE BONDS

If you want to succeed you should strike out on new paths rather than travel the worn paths of accepted success.
—John D. Rockefeller

To be proficient in international trade one must not only understand contracts and documentary credits but must also learn to use to his or her advantage bank guarantees and standby letters of credit. This part of the book introduces this topic and gives samples of most commonly used bank guarantees under ICC rules.

A standby letter of credit or bank guarantee is the other side of the coin from a documentary credit. A documentary letter of credit represents a payment instrument while the guarantee is an assurance that contractual obligations will be fulfilled.

Developed originally in the United States, a standby letter of credit is an undertaking by a bank to pay, which may or may not be conditional upon any other event. The conditions expressed in the letter may stipulate that a certificate of non-performance by an independent inspector or by the beneficiary be provided. Where the bank's promise is to pay the stipulated sum upon request without conditions, the credit is popularly referred to as a "first demand" guarantee.

In 1994, the International Chamber of Commerce released new rules governing demand guarantees payable on first demand. The new rules are intended to encourage uniformity of practice. The ICC rules apply only if expressly stated in the guarantee. Under the Uniform Rules for Demand Guarantees (ICC Publ. No. 458), the beneficiary of a guarantee can assert a claim under the guarantee only by providing a special statement. In particular, the beneficiary has to confirm the occurrence of a breach of contract and to state in what respect the contractual obligations have been violated.

The most common types of guarantees are bid and performance bonds, and advance payment guarantees.

TENDER GUARANTEE/BID BOND

"Tender Guarantee" refers to a guarantee usually given by a bank or insurance company (the "Guarantor") at the request of a tenderer (the "Principal") to a party inviting tenders (the "Beneficiary"), whereby the guarantor undertakes - in the event of default by the Principal in his obligations which results in the submission of the tender - to make payment to the Beneficiary an amount within the limits of a stated sum of money.

Sample Wording of Tender Guarantee

Name of Issuing Bank   (beneficiary = buyer)

Bid Bond No. _____
We have been informed that Messrs _____ (hereinafter called "the Bidder") have submitted to you on _____ under your tender No _____ of _____ their bid for the supply of _____ at a total price _____

According to your tender conditions, the Bidder is required to provide you with a bid bond in the amount of _____

This being stated, we _____ (name of Issuing Bank), _____ (address), irrespective of the validity and the legal effects of the above-mentioned contract and waiving all rights of objection and defense arising from the principal debt, hereby irrevocably undertake to pay immediately to you, upon your first demand, any amount up to

(currency / maximum amount) (in full letters; _____)

upon receipt of your written request for payment and your written confirmation stating that you have accepted, in whole or in part, the above-mentioned bid and that the Bidder is in breach of his obligation(s) under the tender conditions owing to the occurrence of one or more of the following conditions, specifying that:

a) the Bidder has withdrawn its bid during the period of bid validity specified by the bidder on the bid form, or

b) the Bidder has failed to sign the contract awarded to it although it corresponds to the terms of the offer, or

c) the Bidder has failed to furnish the performance bond to be issued upon signature of the awarded contract.

For the purpose of identification, your request for payment and your confirmation have to be presented through the intermediary of a first rate bank confirming that the signatures are legally binding upon your firm. If, in this respect, such bank will make use of tested telex, SWIFT, or tested cable, it will have to transmit in any case the full wording of your request for payment and of your above-mentioned written confirmation and to confirm at the same time that the originals of these documents, legally binding upon your firm, have been for-warded to us.

Our guarantee is valid until _____ and expires in full and automatically, irrespective of whether the present document is returned to us or not, should your written request for payment and your above-mentioned written confirmation or the above-described tested telex, SWIFT, or tested cable sent by the bank not be in our possession by that date at our counters in _____

With each payment under this guarantee our obligation will be reduced pro rata.

This guarantee is subject to the Uniform Rules for Demand Guarantee, ICC Publication No.458.

(Place, date)   Name of Issuing Bank

Authorized Signature

PERFORMANCE GUARANTEE/ PERFORMANCE BOND

"Performance Guarantee" refers to a guarantee usually given by a bank or insurance company (the "Guarantor") at the request of a supplier of goods and services or other contractor (the "Principal"), whereby the Guarantor undertakes - in the event of default by the Principal in due performance of the terms of a contract - to make payment to the Beneficiary an amount within the limits of a stated sum of money, or if the Guarantee so provides, at the guarantor's option, to arrange for performance of the contract.

Sample Wording of Performance Guarantee

Name of Issuing Bank   (Beneficiary = buyer)

Performance Guarantee No _____
We have been informed that you have concluded on _____ a contract No _____ (hereinafter called the "Contract") with Messrs _____ (hereinafter called the "Principal") for the supply of _____ at a total price of _____. According to the Contract, the Principal is required to provide you with a performance guarantee in the amount of _____ (_____% of the total price).

This being stated, we, _____ (name of Issuing Bank), _____ (address), irrespective of the validity and the legal effects of the contract and waiving all rights of objection and defense arising from the principal debt, hereby irrevocably undertake to pay immediately to you, upon your first demand, any amount up to

(currency / maximum amount) (in full letters; _____)

upon receipt of your written request for payment and your written confirmation stating that the Principal is in breach of his obligation(s) under the Contract and explaining in which respect the Principal is in breach.

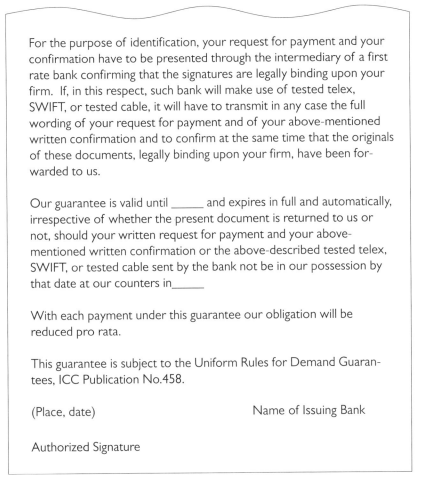

For the purpose of identification, your request for payment and your confirmation have to be presented through the intermediary of a first rate bank confirming that the signatures are legally binding upon your firm. If, in this respect, such bank will make use of tested telex, SWIFT, or tested cable, it will have to transmit in any case the full wording of your request for payment and of your above-mentioned written confirmation and to confirm at the same time that the originals of these documents, legally binding upon your firm, have been forwarded to us.

Our guarantee is valid until _____ and expires in full and automatically, irrespective of whether the present document is returned to us or not, should your written request for payment and your above-mentioned written confirmation or the above-described tested telex, SWIFT, or tested cable sent by the bank not be in our possession by that date at our counters in_____

With each payment under this guarantee our obligation will be reduced pro rata.

This guarantee is subject to the Uniform Rules for Demand Guarantees, ICC Publication No.458.

(Place, date)   Name of Issuing Bank

Authorized Signature

When a new exporter not known to the market is making its first few transactions, importers may ask for a performance bond to back up exporter's obligations under the contract. Such a performance guarantee is usually made in the form of a standby letter of credit.

In case the exporter fails to deliver the goods under a letter of credit or contract, or where performance does not comply with the specifications, the beneficiary of the performance bond has the right to draw an amount as specified by the terms in this standby L/C. The standby L/C is subject to UCPDC500 and is issued for a particular percentage of a total contract (usually 5 to 20 per cent). The wording of such a standby L/C can be more advantageous to the importer or the exporter depending on the terms negotiated between the parties.

If you are issuing a performance bond, you may want to be very specific with regards to documentation needed for the drawing or negotiation of your performance bond. Your objective would be to make it as difficult as possible for the importer to draw on the performance bond in case of default. By doing so, your intent is to protect yourself should an importer decide to take advantage and unscrupulously draw on your performance bond for reasons such as a sudden market downturn. The importer may attempt to claim quality defects in the delivered goods although the goods may be as per specifications detailed in the contract.

In a less than perfect world, business people must be aware and have knowledge of options and opportunities available to them. They must know what they can and cannot do; and what others can and cannot do to them. A trader must know his/her business inside out to avoid the losses which can result from not knowing. It is always better to learn from other people's mistakes than from your own.

As an importer receiving a performance bond you are wise to negotiate a simply worded standby guarantee that would allow you to draw the amount of the bond upon the presentation of a letter on your company letterhead claiming that the exporter failed to meet certain obligations under the contract or L/C. Depending on the wording of a performance bond, which can vary widely, sometimes a simple letter is sufficient to affect the drawing.

Performance bonds can be made to guarantee quality, quantity, timely delivery of goods, to name a few. In the case study, "The vessel named 'Yik Fat'" (Chapter 5), a performance bond is used to guarantee a timely delivery of steel cargo to a Korean mill. The study demonstrates how the exporter, by being more familiar with performance bonds than the importer, was able to protect himself against a force majeure situation that developed during the transaction.

ADVANCE PAYMENT GUARANTEE

"Advance Payment Guarantee" refers to a guarantee usually given by a bank or insurance company (the "Guarantor") at the request of a supplier of goods or services or other contractor (the "Principal") whereby the Guarantor undertakes - in the event of default by the Principal, on repaying in accordance with the terms and conditions of a contract between the Principal and the Beneficiary (the "Contract") any sum or sums advanced or paid by the Beneficiary to the Principal and not otherwise repaid - to make payment to the Beneficiary an amount within the limits of a stated sum of money.

Sample Advance Payment Guarantee

Advance Payment Guarantee No. _____

We have been informed that you have concluded on _____ a contract No _____ (hereinafter called the "Contract") with Messrs _____ (hereinafter called the "Principal") for the supply of _____ at a total price of _____ . According to the contract, you are required to make an advance payment to the Principal of _____ (_____ % of the total price). Your claim for reimbursement of this amount, should the Principal fail to supply the goods in conformity with the terms of the Contract, is to be secured by a bank guarantee.

This being stated, we, _____(name of issuing bank) _____ (address), irrespective of the validity and the legal effects of the Contract and waiving all rights of objection and defence arising from the principal debt, hereby irrevocably undertake to pay immediately to you, upon your first demand, any amount up to

(currency / maximum amount) (in full letters: _____)

upon receipt of your written request for payment and your written confirmation stating that the Principal is in breach of his obligation(s) under the Contract because he has failed to supply the goods in conformity with the terms of the Contract (such terms to be cited) and that, as a result thereof, you are entitled to claim reimbursement of your advance payment.

The present indemnity will enter into force only after receipt of the above-mentioned advance payment of the Principal.

For the purpose of identification, your request for payment and your confirmation have to be presented through the intermediary of a first rate bank confirming that the signatures are legally binding upon your firm. If, in this respect, such bank will make use of tested telex, SWIFT, or tested cable, it will have to transmit in any case the full wording of your request for payment and of your above-mentioned written confirmation and to confirm at the same time that the originals of these documents, legally binding upon your firm, have been forwarded to us.

Our guarantee is valid until _____ and expires in full and automatically, irrespective of whether the present document is returned to us or not, should your written request for payment and your above-mentioned written confirmation or the above-described tested telex, SWIFT, or tested cable sent by the bank not be in our possession by that date at our counters in_____

With each payment under this guarantee our obligation will be reduced pro rata.

This guarantee is subject to the Uniform Rules for Demand Guarantees, ICC Publication No.458.

(Place, date)   Name of Issuing Bank

Authorized Signature

STANDBY LETTER OF CREDIT

Most standby letters of Credit can not be transferred or assigned to another party. In many cases banks would require 100 per cent cash collateral or an established credit line prior to issuing a standby letter of credit.

The standby is a very convenient instrument and if structured properly can give a supplier 100 per cent assurance that in case the buyer fails to pay, the bank which issued the standby credit will pay upon receipt of documents presented.

In the example of a standby letter of credit reprinted below the buyer/applicant issues a guarantee to the supplier/beneficiary covering a purchase of three forty-foot containers of doors. The supplier can draw on the guarantee providing the buyer fails to pay within thirty days after the release of the container(s) to its forwarder.

Example: Standby Letter of Credit (Name of Beneficiary is Fictional)

```
ROYAL BANK OF CANADA
INTL. TRADE CENTRE - ONTARIO
180 WELLINGTON ST. W. 9TH FLOOR
TORONTO, ONTARIO M5J 1J1
CANADA

DATE OF ISSUE:                    OUR REFERENCE NUMBER:

EXPIRY DATE:
PLACE OF EXPIRY:                  TORONTO, ONTARIO

BENEFICIARY:                      APPLICANT:
INTERNATIONAL DOOR LTD.           KORSHUN CORPORATION
1800 WOODWORTH ROAD               2727 STEELES AVE. W.,
TORONTO, ONTARIO,                 TORONTO, ONTARIO,
CANADA                            CANADA
```

AMOUNT: USD 80,720.57 (EIGHTY THOUSAND SEVEN
HUNDRED TWENTY AND 57/ 100 U.S. DOLLARS).

IRREVOCABLE STANDBY LETTER OF CREDIT NO. P0345T1497

WE HEREBY ISSUE IN YOUR FAVOUR THIS IRREVOCABLE LETTER OF CREDIT WHICH IS AVAILABLE BY PAYMENT AGAINST YOUR WRITTEN DEMAND, ADDRESSED TO ROYAL BANK OF CANADA, INTERNATIONAL TRADE CENTRE - ONTARIO, 180 WELLINGTON STREET WEST, TORONTO, ONTARIO M5J 1J1 BEARING THE CLAUSE: "DRAWN UNDER STANDBY LETTER OF CREDIT P0345T1497 ISSUED BY ROYAL BANK OF CANADA, INTERNATIONAL TRADE CENTRE - ONTARIO, 180 WELLINGTON STREET WEST, TORONTO, ONTARIO M5J 1J1," WHEN ACCOMPANIED BY THE FOLLOWING DOCUMENTS:

1 TWO COPIES OF INVOICE(S)

2 BENEFICIARY'S SIGNED CERTIFICATE SPECIFYING AMOUNT CLAIMED AND STATING THAT THE AMOUNT DRAWN REPRESENTS INVOICE(S) VALUE WHICH REMAINS UNPAID BY KORSHUN CORPO- RATION FOR OVER 30 DAYS.

3 COPY OF WAREHOUSE RECEIPT STATING THAT CONTAINERS WITH DOORS HAVE BEEN RELEASED TO THE APPLICANT'S FORWARDER.

4 THE ORIGINAL OF THIS LETTER OF CREDIT FOR OUR ENDORSEMENT OF ANY PAYMENT.

PARTIAL DRAWINGS ARE PERMITTED.

EXCEPT AS OTHERWISE EXPRESSLY STATED THIS CREDIT IS ISSUED SUBJECT TO UNIFORM CUSTOMS AND PRACTICE FOR DOCUMENTARY CREDIT, 1993 REVISION, I.C.C. PUBLICATION NO. 500.

WE ENGAGE TO HONOUR PRESENTATIONS SUBMITTED WITHIN THE TERMS AND CONDITIONS INDICATED ABOVE.

ROYAL BANK OF CANADA

AUTHORIZED SIGNATURE   AUTHORIZED SIGNATURE

Chapter IV

TRADER'S KNOW HOW

Knowledge is to understand that you know something when you do, and to admit that you do not know something when you do not.

— *Confucius*

Chapter 4 is designed to give the reader practical trading knowledge about international marketing; cultural fundamentals of trading; risks associated with Free on Board (FOB) terms; obtaining exclusive rights; understanding the advantages and disadvantages in being a commissions agent versus a trading house; managing currency fluctuations; and the importance of a face-to-face meeting.

Through the use of case studies, Chapter 5 goes further in illustrating other practical aspects and understanding of international trade. It is always better to learn from other peoples' mistakes than from your own.

The author hopes that the reader will avoid pitfalls if faced with similar situations as discussed herein.

FIRST STEPS TO TRADING

- Find a country where a product can be purchased at a low price, and find a place to sell that product at a higher price.

- Know the laws and regulations of both the country from where you are buying and to where you are selling the product.

- Make a contract which clearly specifies the responsibilities of the buyer and seller and leaves as little doubt as possible as to the actions to be taken by both parties.

A trader can be successful without money, but he or she cannot be successful without a sound knowledge of products, markets, and international rules and regulations.

INTERNATIONAL MARKETING

One of the first major issues you must face is deciding who exactly your market is. What type of individual and what type of business constitutes the natural target audience for the product you seek to import and sell?

Another question you must answer is: where is your market located? You will have to define the geographic location of your potential market.

- Who needs your product and why?
- What makes your product different and desirable?
- Where do you find the people who need your product?
- What other product criteria lead to acceptance or rejection?

To be successful as an international trader one should focus on a "country of expertise." Country of expertise refers to a country having a language and culture with which you are familiar. If you are an American citizen of Chinese origin, your country of expertise may be

China, for the reasons mentioned above. On the other hand, if you father's friend from childhood is the Minister of Agriculture of Malaysia, Malaysia might be your country of expertise and you might choose to source agricultural products from the United States and Canada for the Malaysian market.

Traders need to be aware of the time frame to which they are committing themselves in order to achieve a profitable return on their investment. Most successful trading companies have prevailed in foreign markets because of a commitment to the long haul. In fact, many successful companies initially concentrate their efforts on gaining market share before even contemplating profitability. There is no such thing as a short-term fix, and there are very, very few get-rich-quick schemes that work. The fact that foreign traders are often perceived as being motivated by the desire to make a quick killing makes it especially important that companies work twice as hard to allay these perceptions by showing a level of commitment sufficient to sustain the long haul.

Traders must become intimately acquainted with their markets. Getting to know the customer requires analysing trade and economic statistics, studying demographics and buying patterns, and keeping informed of world events that influence the international market place. It is absolutely essential that some effort be made to understand these issues and to focus your marketing strategies accordingly.

It is also essential that traders be willing and able to make personal visits to their foreign markets. Many cultures highly value personal relationships and will not even consider entering into a business arrangement with someone whom they do not know personally. A trader's presence in a foreign country will send a strong message of commitment to local business.

Once you have decided to do business in a foreign market, the next consideration should be how the goods will be distributed in that market. Distribution channels are of paramount importance because they represent the lifeline between the seller and the buyer.

The problem of finding suitable channels of distribution is often complicated by a foreign environment, but it is still critical to find the best means for your needs. Most countries support many trade services such as export management companies, export trading companies, and commission agents.

The degree of challenge in finding effective distribution channels will largely depend on whether a trader sells directly or indirectly to the end user. If a trader decides to sell indirectly the risks and complexities associated with foreign trade are somewhat less, but the level of control over and contact with foreign markets is also reduced. By selling directly, the exporter retains greater control over the process, can personally meet customers, and need not pay out a percentage of the sale price. As one would expect, with the potential for greater dividends comes greater responsibility and risk. Selling directly to the market requires a trader to select the best channels of distribution, which can be a difficult task. The channels of distribution generally include agents, distributors, sales representatives, retailers, and partners. In some countries they perform identical or overlapping functions; in others their roles are quite different.

Many businesspeople find that selling in foreign markets is much easier through a local agent or representative. An agent will generally represent and act on behalf of a company in a foreign country.

Eight items the trader must remember when marketing internationally:

1. Keep in touch with your most important customers and contacts. Personal contact is critical to building a business relationship.

2. Send samples of your products.

3. Distribute catalogues, brochures, flyers, and technical information to potential buyers.

4. Respect cultural differences, and adapt your product and marketing as needed. These latter must also be in line with government regulations.

5. Concentrate efforts on a specific market or region, work to build lasting relationships and repeat business there, and then expand as your products gain their own reputation.

6. Follow up on initial sales inquiries. Establish a person who will be responsible for working with a client from the start to finish of a transaction.

7. Price your product to fit the market. Don't underprice your merchandise. Know what your competitors are doing in that same market and surrounding markets.

8. Deliver on time. The Americans have an expression "Just in time delivery." Learn and follow it.

Contacts is the first and last word in international trade. If you can build contacts and understand transferable credits and assignments of proceeds you are in business.

EXCLUSIVE RIGHTS

It is often said that if a trader obtains exclusive rights to a product he is close to success. There are debates over whether or not exclusive rights to a product should be bought. Many traders maintain, as a rule of thumb, that one should never pay for such rights. The reasoning behind this conviction is that the trading companies promote products in foreign markets where producers would not venture on their own. The trader invests time and money taking all the risks himself. In most cases the producer does not invest a single penny in the foreign market and the trading company must often absorb the losses where a product fails to be accepted. For these reasons, the trading company should not pay for exclusive rights.

Often a producer does not want to give a blanket exclusive right to one trading company, particularly in a large market, such as the United States, Europe, Asia, and so forth. The reason for this is obvious. The producer is not sure of the performance of the trading company and does not want to "put all its eggs in one basket." The trading company would be wise to counter these reservations by saying to the producer, "Yes, you are absolutely right to be cautious about our performance. You don't want to be in a situation where your factory has committed its export production to us, and we are not performing up to your expectations. Therefore, we suggest that you specify, in an exclusive rights agreement, the minimum quantity of product we must sell in order to maintain exclusivity in marketing your products in a specific market. If for any reason we fail to meet the agreed expectations, you would have the full legal right to break the contract with our company and seek a better partner." At the same time, a trader must communicate to the supplier that he is aggressive, knowledgeable, and has experience in the export market for which the exclusive rights are asked.

Manufacturers often make the mistake of entering a new market through a variety of channels and without structured export prices. They themselves try to sell factory-direct to any buyer who approaches them and at the same time they employ traders who have expertise in a particular market. Soon many prices are floating in the market for

91

the same product and as a result, the end buyer becomes cautious about making a purchase. By being too greedy, manufacturers can thus end up "shooting themselves in the foot."

In markets such as Russia, China, Middle East, South America, and others, agents and local trading companies play a very important role in facilitating trade. The trader who speaks the same language as the buyer is better able to communicate all the advantages of doing business with one producer or manufacturer of foreign goods rather than another. It often all comes down to having relationships and personal contacts with the right people who are able to make the decisions. Traders who have a good name in a local market are the ones that get the business.

Sometimes a trading company is more important than the manufacturer it represents. For these reasons, manufacturers who want to penetrate a new export market must study the needs of the market and locate the right partner/trader or traders who would work locally with the end buyers and provide product support, information, and service. Exclusive right agreements may be signed for a small territory and then expanded if a trader is successful. Sometimes exclusive rights are given for a specific region or clearly identifiable geographic location.

There are many forms of exclusive rights agreements. Some are lengthy, legal documents, others are only a few pages long. Usually, the more specific the agreement, the better it is for the trader, providing the details of the agreement cover the trader's rights to unconditional exclusivity. The same can be said for the other side. A manufacturer may want to include in the agreement many points under which it may break the agreement. As the trader's profit margin is usually higher than the manufacturers, once a new market is penetrated, there is a danger that the local distributors or end buyers will find out who the producer is, and try to approach them directly to avoid paying the higher price from a trading company. The term "going behind the back" is familiar to all traders who have experienced this phenomenon.

The case study "Exclusive Rights – How to get them, how to protect them" in Chapter 5 discusses the challenges encountered in structuring exclusive rights agreements.

COMMISSION AGENT VS. TRADING HOUSE

When you tell people that you are a trader, the word that springs to mind for most of them is "middleman." For many traders, the term middleman has negative connotations.

What is a middleman? A middleman is not a principal in a transaction. He is an agent who works for a particular buyer, seller, or both, putting the deal together and receiving a commission as compensation for the services rendered. An agent usually signs a commission's agreement with either the buyer, seller, or both and helps to negotiate the particulars of contracts, letters of credit, and shipment details between the parties. In some cases, once the agent puts the two parties together and business starts rolling, the buyer, supplier, or both may feel that the agent's use has expired. If commissions payable to the agent are substantial, the employer may want to break the relationship. As the saying goes "I made my money by cutting out the middleman." Nobody likes a middleman, however, exporters and importers who are experienced and well established in the business will tell you that a good agent, especially when selling into a foreign country, is a priceless asset.

Agents do not accept letters of credits in their favour, but they help negotiate contract terms between the buyer and seller directly. If an agent accepts a letter of credit in his/her favour and starts acting as a principal, then it is time to change titles from "agent" to "trading house."

Although it is true that trading houses sometimes act as agents, the primary difference between the two is that the trader is a principal who cannot be cut out of the deal whereas the agent is truly a middleman.

THE FACE-TO-FACE MEETING

"However sophisticated our communications media,
a face-to-face meeting makes the most impression.
Words are reinforced by body language and gesture.
Face-to-face meetings between influential politicians
can change the course of history. The same is true of trade.
You can do business by phone, fax and computer screen,
but sometimes you need to be on the spot to negotiate the best
deal, strengthen personal links or check the quality of the goods."
Mees Pierson N.V.

In international trade a relationship between two people can be the most important factor in success. You must be able to build relationships with all kinds of people, preferably the ones that you like. Face-to-face meetings are very important and should not be overlooked despite today's high technology communication age. Trading is still very much a people business. Trust or no trust in a trader can make or break a transaction.

On a business trip to London, England, the agent for a company that I was working for at the time met me at Heathrow Airport and drove me back to the hotel. In the car we discussed business and once in the hotel the agent pulled out a draft of the letter of credit and asked me to accept the terms so he could go back to the buyer and conclude the sales contract on our behalf. The agent was to receive $10,000 commission if the deal was successfully concluded. The terms of the letter of credit were very rigid and normally I would not have accepted them. In this case, however, the agent assured me that if there were discrepancies in our documents as presented under the letter of credit, the buyer would give the issuing bank instructions to accept such discrepancies and would not hold up payment. I accepted the agent's assurances based on my personal relationship with this person and my trust in his past performance. I was confident in his ability to put this deal together.

The face-to-face meeting that day was used more to the agent's advantage. At the end of the day, however, we were both working towards a common goal that was eventually achieved. One month later when the documents were presented with discrepancies, as I thought might happen, the buyer held up payment for more than one week claiming he needed to get approval from top management in order to accept the documents as presented. At the end of the week I told the agent that I had accepted such L/C conditions only based on his word and asked him to push the buyer to release payment immediately. The next day, the issuing bank telexed our negotiating bank that the buyer had accepted the documents with discrepancies and that payment would be affected within three working days. Our company discounted the L/C for those three days and the deal was closed. I wondered if I had made the right decision in accepting terms and conditions of the credit that I knew our company would have difficulty meeting. I came to the conclusion that I should have negotiated more flexible terms. But if I knew yesterday what I now know today, I would spend all day at the race track.

CULTURAL FUNDAMENTALS OF TRADING

It is important to realise the cultural framework within which you are trading. Seeing things from the point of view of another culture will help you become more receptive to the differences. It is necessary to know that your own cultural background is influencing how you look at a situations, and how a foreign counterpart sees you. Recognizing and understanding this can help in your goal of obtaining a successful result.

Do not push your identity on others. When in a foreign culture do not insist on doing things the way you do them in your home country. At the same time, do not try to become one of them. You may lose their respect.

Pay attention to etiquette. Etiquette is entrenched in many cultures and by showing respect for social and business etiquette you are showing respect for your trading partners. It is important to learn at least something about the local etiquette of both business and social occasions. Such things as personal space, physical contact, gestures, and gift giving may differ from country to country.

Try not to judge the cultural preferences of your counterpart. There may be aspects of another culture that you do not like or agree with. To the extent that your opinions are based on personal experience or first-hand knowledge, you must handle these cultural differences with the same tact that you would utilize with domestic business associates you do not particularly care for. However, make every effort to overcome perceptions that are based on unfounded biases.

Not knowing the local language can be one of the biggest obstacles to trading in foreign countries. Try to learn the language if possible. Use the services of professional interpreters who preferably have some knowledge of the topic being discussed. Be aware of the ambiguity of language - what you say and what is understood is not always the same thing. There are three points in a conversation where a misunderstanding can take place. First, you may not have thought through completely what you wanted to say and thus have not said what you meant. Second, you may have said what you meant, but the person may not have heard exactly what you said. Third, the person may have heard exactly what you said but may not have understood completely what you meant.

Pay attention to body language. Gestures and body movement are important means of communicating, and some familiarity with the local ways of expression will go far in recognizing and interpreting unspoken messages.

Although research is an important way to learn about another culture there is no substitute for visiting a country to experience its culture in person. Face-to-face meetings will help you and your customer build trust and mutual respect for each other.

Sometimes seemingly minor actions can have a major impact and even the slightest attempt to get along will bring disproportionately positive results. Pay attention to:

- Level of eye and physical contact.
- Posture.
- Gifts to bring to parties and other social occasions.
- Having some knowledge about the country you are visiting.

Customs are deeply rooted cultural issues that are quite important to nationals of certain countries. One must be aware of the following:

- Eating habits and mealtimes. These may vary significantly from culture to culture and people can be offended by habits different from their own.
- Work hours and holidays.
- Drinking and toasting rules when attending parties, social, or business gatherings.
- Gender behaviour.
- Religious observances and festivals.

There are many peculiarities about different cultures that are not quite rules, or customs, but that are nonetheless noticeable social patterns. Some observations might include:

- How much business takes place at the first meeting, and how important are business cards?
- Whether business continues during a meal after a meeting, or whether you should just enjoy the social occasion.
- National pride.
- Body language.

Negotiations and negotiating styles are absolutely critical to the success or failure of a foreign business endeavour. Yet these vary so widely even within cultures that it is difficult to pinpoint specific rules or recommendations. There are, however, some important points to remember when negotiating:

- Avoid outright conflict with foreign business associates.
- Do not haggle over the price unless this is commonplace in the culture.
- Avoid shifts in conversation tone or in negotiating style.
- Try to find out if the client will negotiate a lower price no matter what the initial offer is, or if the client will be offended if the price first offered will not be subject to other offers. For cultures that love to negotiate perhaps a better strategy would be to start with a higher price and give them the satisfaction of making you accept a lower price.

You must always judge a situation on its own merits. Never assume anything unless there are facts to back up your opinion. One comforting thought is that in all cultures, business has the same goal, to make money. This desire transcends most other cultural and religious differences.

MANAGING CURRENCY EXCHANGE FLUCTUATIONS

One of the uncertainties in international trade is the fluctuation of exchange rates among currencies. The relative value between the buyer's currency and the seller's currency may change in the time from when the deal is made until payment is received. A devaluation or rise in one currency against another can cause either a win or a loss to one party or the other involved in the transaction.

A way to avoid this type of risk is to quote prices and establish payment in the currency of your own country. This is practical with freely convertible and stable currencies. Therefore, U.S. dollars, German marks, English pounds, Japanese yen, French francs, and Swiss francs are often quoted.

Foreign exchange, often referred to as FOREX, is defined as claims payable in a foreign country in a foreign currency. As a rule, traders operate using their own national currencies, money recognized and legally acceptable for transactions within the particular currency zone. For example, a seller/exporter in Japan usually wants to be paid in his or her own currency, the yen (¥), rather than in that of the importer, who, if he is from the United States, may want to use U.S. dollars (US$). However, the seller may on occasion prefer to be paid in English pounds (GBP) in order to pay off obligations due to a British company in that currency.

A currency that can be readily exchanged for another is known as a convertible currency. If it can be fully, readily, and legally converted under virtually all circumstances, a currency is referred to as being unrestricted. Many countries maintain restricted convertibility on their currencies, often allowing full convertibility only for nonresidents while limiting the ability of residents to exchange domestic for foreign currencies. Other countries have inconvertible currencies, which cannot legally be taken out of the country or exchanged for foreign currencies. However, other countries distinguish between foreign exchange involving current transactions (for goods and services) and those involving capital investments, with freedom of convertibility being restricted to some degree for one category or the other. Such a situation may result in what is known as a two-tier market, in which access to restricted currency is controlled. Exchange controls rationing foreign currency can block imports into the country and can create a black market trade in currencies and commodities.

Currencies & Exchange Rates

Hard currencies are those of large, strong economies that have few if any restrictions on the use and exchange of their currencies, while soft currencies are those for which there is little or no demand due to restrictions on free exchange. International financial operations are usually transacted using key currencies, that is, those that are relatively strong, broadly convertible, and generally accepted. They are sometimes referred to as reserve currencies, and most international business is transacted using or at least with reference to these currencies.

The exchange rate is simply the amount of a nation's currency that can be bought at a given time for a specified amount of the currency of another country. For example, DM/$=1.70 means that one US dollar would be equal to 1.70 German marks. The exchange rate is given either as a direct quote, expressed as the number of units of a foreign currency per US$ (DM/$), or as an indirect quote, expressed as the number of US$ per unit of foreign currency ($/DM), which is the reciprocal of the first quote. Since the US$ is the most commonly traded currency, international foreign exchange transactions are usually quoted directly using the US$ as the reference point.

This necessitates the use of cross-rates, in which currencies are not compared directly with each other but in terms of a reference currency which serves as a common denominator. In order to find the rate for the GBP/DM, you must first have quotes on both currencies in US$, then use them to calculate the rate for GBP/DM with reference to the common dollar rates of each. Forex traders quote bid and ask price ranges, with the first figure always that at which they stand ready to buy currencies and the second figure that at which they are willing to sell. This difference constitutes the spread, or base profit margin, for the institution. Currency traders deal not in full quotes but in a shorthand, referred to as pips or ticks. These are the last decimal places in a quote, usually 1/100th, or .001, of a per cent. Currency traders are assumed to know the base rates and deal only in the marginal fluctuations.

A series of conversions may allow for the possibility of arbitrage, which involves taking advantage of temporal and spatial anomalies in pricing in the international currency markets. If the German bank's price on SwF is less than the Swiss bank can get for them in Singapore, it will buy SwF from the German bank and immediately sell them to the Singapore bank to make a profit on the price differential. However, because virtually all international currency transactions are quoted against the US$ and instant communications and twenty-four hour trading compensate for distance and time differences, the opportunities for such arbitrage are few.

The relative value of currencies depends on a variety of economic and political factors, but the key factor is supply and demand for a particular currency. The main economic factor is the equilibrium rate, or purchasing power parity, at which goods would cost the same in each country. This ignores many important factors, such as quality, exportability, and long-term capital flow issues, but serves as a useful approximation of the relative strength of currencies against each other. If the same amount of currency in country "A" buys the same goods as an equivalent amount of currency in country "B," the currencies are at parity. If the same amount of currency buys more goods in country "A" than in country "B" then the currency of country "A" is undervalued and/or that of country "B" is overvalued.

Countries try to manage their currencies to maintain stable exchange rates against those of their trading partners. Central banks of respective countries may attempt to maintain a fixed exchange rate in which the value of their currency is linked to a commodity, such as gold, or to another strong currency, such as the US$. When a currency is linked directly to that of a stronger country, it is said to be pegged to that of the stronger country whose lead it follows. The nations of the world have generally been unable to maintain such fixed rates in the volatile and increasingly integrated global economy of the twentieth century, leading to the use of floating rates.

Floating exchange systems rely on a variety of mechanisms to set actual prices. The main ones involve trade-weighted rates that hinge on the degree of importance of a given country's trade with the nation. A variation of this is to use a basket of currencies in which the exchange rate is figured in proportion to the value of the various currencies among the designated countries

Most foreign exchange trading results from the need to acquire foreign currency for a specific trade transaction. If the conversion is for use in a current transaction, it occurs in the spot market at the current price, or spot rate, for immediate delivery (within two business days). If the foreign exchange is required for a future transaction, it occurs in the forward market for future delivery. The difference between the prices in the spot and forward markets is due to the relative levels of interest rates in the two countries. If a currency is actually held by the party, it can earn interest between now and when it is needed at prevailing money market rates. Conversely, it must be borrowed at a cost commensurate with the value of the interest earnings foregone by the lender. So the forward price will include the amount of interest that could be earned during the period, usually making forward rates higher than spot rates because of this premium.

Futures & Options

The ability to buy forward foreign exchange allows businesses to hedge their risks by counterbalancing a current transaction through a similar future transaction to offset the effects of price changes during the interim. In currency trading this is often accomplished through a swap, the spot purchase or sale of foreign exchange and a simultaneous forward sale or purchase of the same currency. A spot purchase combined with a future sale is called an outward swap, while a spot sale connected to a forward purchase is an inward swap. A forward purchase or sale not covered by an offsetting spot transaction is known as an outright transaction. Actual holdings of a currency are known as long positions, while those with uncovered future positions are called short positions or are said to be short of exchange.

Options contracts allow foreign exchange traders the right to buy (call) or sell (put) specified quantities of currencies at a point in the future. If an option is in the money — that is, the actual price is above the exercise price and therefore the option is profitable — it can be exercised. If it is out of the money — the exercise price is below the actual price and therefore the option is unprofitable — it can be allowed to expire. Options traders seldom if ever take delivery of the actual currencies but simply close out the profitable contracts for the amount of the profit. Contracts known as American options can be exercised at any time during the life of the contract, while European options can only be exercised on the expiration date.

Global Currency Markets

Most foreign exchange trading involves financial institutions trading for their own accounts rather than straight business transactions on behalf of clients. Such activity serves to add depth and liquidity to the FOREX market. Because of the large turnover in self-liquidating transactions, many of which are highly leveraged, the nominal dollar value of the volume of such trade far outstrips that of the underlying economic and monetary base that supports it. Major foreign exchange markets are run out of New York, London, Frankfurt, Amsterdam, Singapore, Hong Kong, and Tokyo, but traders can operate anywhere thanks to modern communications links. Trading is most active during the business hours in these respective locations, but can occur anytime.

Euromarkets—consisting of informal markets to deal in transactions involving a currency outside of its country of origin—provide offshore international access to funds unencumbered by governmental regulation. London, Frankfurt, Zurich, and Amsterdam are the main centres of this trade. The Asian dollar market, operating primarily out of Singapore, is also growing rapidly.

Understanding the risks of currency fluctuations and taking advantage of opportunities through the use of hedging, options, and futures will make you a better trader. The most important thing to remember as a trader is that you must conclude a contract with your supplier in the same currency as the contract with your buyer. I remember when our trading company issued a letter of credit to a Japanese car manufacturer in Japanese Yen for three 4x4 jeeps which we sold in US Dollars. When the contract was signed one US$ bought 125¥; when it came time to pay for the jeeps two months later after they were produced and ready for shipment, the Japanese currency appreciated and one US$ now bought only 115¥. On a US$60,000 contract originally budgeted at 125¥ (L/C issued for 7,500,000¥), our trading company had to pay additional US$5,217.39 for the difference in the exchange rate, 115-125¥. The profit which was supposed to result from this deal, US$5000, translated into a loss of US$217.39. Had our trading company purchased the Japanese Yen forward two months at the time of L/C issuance, the profit margin would have been retained.

RISKS OF SELLING FOB AND HOW TO MINIMIZE THEM

When dealing in goods such as steel, fertilizer, grains, and other products which require transportation by a vessel, a trader often tries to purchase goods on FOB terms and in turn sell them on CFR or CIF terms. There are advantages and disadvantages to FOB terms depending from whose side you are analysing the transaction, the buyer's or the seller's.

From the seller's side, FOB terms entail arranging transportation from the production facility to the port of loading, as well as arranging with the local freight forwarder terms and conditions of loading. The latter usually requires that the goods be stowed, lashed, secured, and dunnaged, abbreviated on most contracts as FOB ST. L/S/D.

Stowage: The placing of goods in a ship in such a way as to ensure, first, the safety and stability of the ship not only on a sea or ocean passage but also in between ports when parts of the cargo have been loaded or discharged, as the case may be; second, the safety of the individual consignments which should not be damaged or contaminated by goods being in proximity to goods with which they are not compatible; third, the ability to unload goods at their port of discharge without having to move goods destined for other ports.

Lash: To hold goods in position by the use of, for example, wires, ropes, chains or straps. Devices, such as those listed, used to secure a cargo on a ship, truck, or railway car, or inside a shipping container.

Secure: To prevent a cargo from shifting in transit, usually by lashing it to the ship or to the container or vehicle by means of wires, chains, ropes, or straps.

Dunnage: Materials of various types, often timber or matting, placed among the cargo for separation and hence protection from damage, for ventilation and, in the case of certain cargoes, to provide a space in which the forks of a forklift truck may be inserted.

The seller's responsibility under FOB terms ends when goods have crossed the ship's rail and have been loaded on board, L/S/D, if required by the sales contract. The seller must also pay for loading costs, if not included in carriage charge, and fulfil all export customs formalities. By the time the goods arrive at the dock, the seller is still financing the value of the goods and forwarding costs. This means that the buyer has probably not paid for the goods and at best has issued an irrevocable letter of credit for the FOB value of the goods. Where selling terms are FOB, most letters of credit are negotiated against the following documents:

- Commercial invoice.
- Full set of Clean on Board Ocean Bills of Lading marked 'freight collect.'
- Certificate of Origin.
- Beneficiary's certificate stating that a full set of non-negotiable documents will be sent to the buyer by courier service within ten days after shipment.
- SGS quality/quantity certificate, or producer's quality certificate (depending on the product and the trust between the buyer and seller).

The seller will have no problem obtaining and preparing the export documentation listed above with one exception. He may have difficulty getting the ORIGINAL FULL SET OF BILLS OF LADING within the latest shipment date listed in accordance with the respective letter of credit. If the buyer does not nominate a vessel within the time specified in the documentary credit and then fails to extend the L/C, the seller is stuck with the material in the port of loading, paying storage costs. If this happens, the only option the seller has is to sue for breach of contract and look for another buyer for the goods. Such scenarios are common when there is a decline in the market.

Traders who like to take open positions in the market usually prefer to buy on FOB terms. An open position refers to purchasing a product that a trader plans to resell at a later date without having a buyer on the other side to cover the purchase. For example, a steel trader may buy steel billets for shipment in three months time, without having a buyer at the time of the purchase. The steel trader essentially buys on the speculation that the market will go up and he will be able to make a profit.

The most obvious reason and the one that traders often give for preferring FOB terms is that those terms give them the flexibility to work in the freight market and charter vessels. Depending on supply and demand in the freight market, a few thousand dollars can be made by negotiating a better freight rate for the goods. If an opportunity arises to find a vessel that can combine loading your cargo with other cargo in a particular load port or neighbouring ports, then even greater savings can result. Purchasing FOB also gives the buyer greater freedom to sell the product in a market of his choice providing there are no restrictions from the producer of the goods, an export license is readily available, and there are no dumping regulations in the country of import.

The not-so-obvious reason, and the one that traders will not often divulge, is that buying FOB gives them an opportunity to get out of a deal if the market turns against them or for any other reason. Even if an irrevocable L/C is issued in favour of the seller, it does not guarantee payment if the credit calls for a full set of Bills of Lading (B/L). By not presenting a vessel to load the material presented under the contract, the buyer effectively forces the L/C to expire unutilized. The seller can prepare all other documents required under the letter of credit aside from the bill of lading, unless he charters a vessel himself and sends the goods to the destination mentioned in the L/C. This is rarely done, but theoretically and practically it is possible. If the value of goods is substantially high, for example, U.S. $5 million, and the cost to charter a vessel is approximately U.S. $300,000, it may be worth the risk to charter the vessel, get a full set of clean B/L, put all other documentation together, confirm the L/C covering these goods, and then hope that your bank can negotiate the documents successfully. It will be a shock to the buyer when he learns that documents are presented in full compliance with the credit terms and the negotiating bank is claiming reimbursement.

Having received U.S. $5 million the seller will be in a stronger position to negotiate with the "unscrupulous" buyer. Where the seller does not protect himself by other means, there is a risk of non-performance by the buyer in FOB contracts. It is not ethical for traders to behave in such a way and, of course, there are provisions in contracts that penalize such behavior. However, in practice, the only winners in court are the lawyers. In most cases a solution to a commercial dispute is best found by amicable negotiation between the parties.

To help avoid losses for sellers in FOB contracts resulting from buyers not presenting vessels in time to meet the L/C's latest shipment date, a provision in the credit terms can be added calling for presentation of document(s) that can substitute for the full set of clean B/L in the credit's negotiation. Such a document can be a Forwarders Certificate of Receipt (FCR). The FCR can state that goods are located at a specific berth or warehouse in the port of loading, free of all encumbrances, ready to be loaded on board a vessel nominated by the buyer.

The FCR can further state, depending on the L/C requirements, that the goods are customs cleared for export and that all costs relating to loading on board FOB stowed, lashed, secured, and dunnaged are for the account of the seller. In fact this provision keeps both the buyer and seller honest. If the seller does not deliver all the goods, plus or minus the allowable tolerance of 5 to 10 per cent in the time specified in the documentary credit, he cannot negotiate the L/C. On the other hand, however, if the buyer fails to present a vessel in time and the seller has delivered the cargo to port, the seller can use the FCR or other document agreed to in the sales contract to substitute for the B/L and thus can negotiate the L/C.

A sample of a protective FCR clause is reprinted below:

BENEFICIARY CAN DRAW FULL CARGO VALUE AGAINST THE FOLLOWING DOCUMENTS WHICH REPLACE THE BILL OF LADING:

1. FULL SET ORIGINAL FORWARDER'S CERTIFICATE OF RECEIPT MADE OUT TO ORDER OF THE ISSUING BANK INDICATING FULL DESCRIPTION OF GOODS AS PER L/C, NET AND GROSS WEIGHT PER SIZE, AND BERTH NUMBER WHERE THE GOODS ARE HELD.

2. BENEFICIARY'S CERTIFIED COPY OF CARGO READINESS SENT TO APPLICANT VIA FAX/TELEX.

3. BENEFICIARY'S CERTIFICATE ATTESTING THAT THE VESSEL NOMINATED BY APPLICANT HAS FAILED TO ARRIVE AT LOAD PORT WITHIN 21 DAYS AFTER NOTICE OF CARGO READINESS AND THAT ALL CARGO ARE NOW IN PORT READY FOR CUSTOMS CLEARANCE AND LOADING ON BOARD THE VESSEL.

The above clause is worded in a way to protect the buyer and the seller. The buyer is assured that the right quantity and type of goods are delivered to the port. The seller, on the other hand, is confident that if the buyer does not present a vessel within twenty-one days from the date of notice of readiness he will be able to draw the full L/C value against an FCR.

Example: Forwarder's Certificate of Receipt

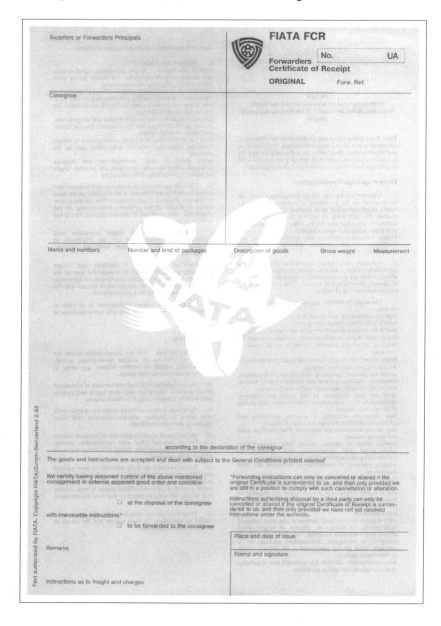

FOUR BASIC RULES OF INTERNATIONAL TRADING

RULE #1 - Buy Low, Sell High

Buy low, sell high, and make the difference in the middle. One successful trader was asked how he made his fortune in the trading business. "Very simple, my dear," he replied, "I added 1 per cent, 2 per cent to the initial purchase price from the manufacturer." "What do you mean by 1 per cent, 2 per cent?" "I bought a product for one dollar, I sold it for two dollars, therefore 1 per cent, 2 per cent."

RULE #2 - Success in International Trade is Defined as Meeting:

- the right people
- at the right place
- at the right time

and a little bit of "mazel" (luck).

RULE #3 - Know the Laws in the Country Where You are Buying, Know the Laws in the Country Where You are Selling

International trade is a game like tennis, golf, basketball, or chess, you must know the rules before you can play.

RULE #4 - Fake It 'Til You Make It

Negotiate with confidence and be calm even when you are put on the spot. Start with what you know. If you don't know, don't guess, say that you don't know but will find out from people in your company who do know, like the technical director.

Chapter V

CASE STUDIES

Action may not always bring happiness; but there is no happiness without action.

—Disraeli

The case studies presented in this part of the book are taken from the real life experiences of the author. They are chosen specifically to reflect on subjects discussed in Chapters: I, II, III, IV. Fax correspondence, contracts, letters of credit, performance bonds, and exclusive rights agreements have been reprinted word for word to give the flavour of the deals as they took place. The names of buyers and suppliers have been replaced by generic terms for the purpose of confidentiality. The aim of these case studies is to give the reader better understanding of how to conduct him/herself in business situations in order to take decisive action with confidence.

CASE STUDY #1
From Hong Kong to Russia – 9000 Telephones

How SGS Quality Inspection Saved the Day.

In October 1991 a Canadian trading company began to negotiate the purchase of 9000 telephone sets built at a factory in China and sold through a Hong Kong trading company.

The cost of each telephone was U.S. $4.00. The Canadian trading company resold these phones to a Russian importer for U.S. $5.00. Total gross profit on the sale of 9000 units was U.S. $9,000.00

The Hong Kong trading company was not previously known to the Canadian trading company. Acting as the principle supplier in the transaction, it was introduced to the Canadian company by the Hong Kong Trade Development Council. The seller was prompt in sending samples of the telephones free of charge via courier, and the price of the phones was competitive for the Russian market at the time.

During fax correspondence the Hong Kong supplier seemed very professional. It was clear that they knew this business and were only involved in trading telephones rather than any item "under the sun," as can sometimes happen with other trading companies.

The Canadian company made its final decision to purchase the phones when the Hong Kong supplier accepted as terms of payment a letter of credit payable at the counters of a Canadian bank, and also accepted an SGS Quality and Quantity Certificate as one of the documents to be presented under the L/C.

Instructions for the paying/accepting/negotiating bank in the letter of credit read: UNLESS OTHERWISE SPECIFIED NEGOTIATING BANK WILL FORWARD ALL DRAFT(S) AND DOCUMENTS TO US (THE ROYAL BANK OF CANADA) IN ONE MAILING. This meant that before payment against the documents presented under the letter of credit, the Royal Bank documentary credit department would make sure that all documents corresponded strictly to the terms and conditions of the letter of credit. If the payment conditions had allowed for payment at the counters of the beneficiary's bank in Hong Kong, it would have given the seller greater leeway in documentary compliance to the letter of credit. In theory banks all over the world follow the same procedure in checking documentary credits using the latest UCPDC 500 regulations; however, in practice, the individuals who check the documents are capable of error and smaller banks in particular may not have sufficient staff to check and double check the documents presented. The personal relationships that the buyer has with the issuing bank and the seller has with the negotiating bank must also be taken into consideration despite all rules and regulations. Regardless of which side of the transaction you are on, it is always better for the documents to be checked by your banker, and for the L/C to be structured such that it is negotiated at your bank's counters.

Accepting the SGS Quality Certificate inside the credit's documents gave the Canadian Buyer confidence that the telephones would be of acceptable quality. If the quality of the phones were not to meet the industry standards, SGS would not issue a Certificate of Quality and the seller would not be able to collect the proceeds under the letter of credit. The quality standards had to be negotiated as the actual copies of fax correspondence between the buyer and the supplier demonstrate. In the end the SGS Certificate of Quality saved the Canadian trading company from a potential quality claim and a possible lawsuit that might have ended up in losses of thousands of dollars.

Copies of actual fax correspondence between the Canadian trading company (CTC) and the Hong Kong supplier (HKTC) are reprinted below:

1. Proforma Invoice from HKTC

TO: CTC - Buyer

DATE: Oct. 17, 1991

Thank you for your fax just received today.

Model No.	Description	Qty.	Unit Price	Amount
CT-900	USSR Standard, Gov additional weight to the base. 60cm (stretch 8 feet) long coil cord from pin to other endings pin	9000 pcs	US$4.00 CIF ST. Petersburg	US$36,000
	Colour: Red 3000 pcs. Black 3000 pcs. Blue 3000 pcs			

Delivery: Before Nov. 15, 1991

Payment: By irrevocable & at sight L/C.

Remarks: (1) SGS inspection level, it must be at our standard for telephone inspection.
(2) Additional weight to the base, extra charge U.S. $0.10
(3) We will supply one more foot of stretch coil cord for you free of charge

Bank: Overseas Trust Bank Ltd., Hong Kong

Best regards, HKTC

2. Reply from CTC

Attn: Export Manager, Supplier Co., HK

Date: October 21, 1991

We received your proforma invoice in good order. Monday morning Toronto time I will give an order to the Royal Bank of Canada to issue a letter of credit in your favour !!!!

1. Please let me know urgently if you can send our container to Odessa port not St Petersburg. What is the sailing date to Odessa?

2. Also please tell us the scheduled sailing date to St. Petersburg .

3. What is the weight of the CT-900 without the extra weight and with the extra weight?

4. Please send to our Toronto Office 4 samples of CT-900 USSR standard with the extra weight and 2 CT-900 American standard with the extra weight for testing in Canada. Please send these samples to us via Federal Express ASAP.

Awaiting your reply, CTC

3. HKTC Fax

To: CTC

Date: October 21, 1991

Thank you for your fax just received today.

1. 12/11 ETA HKG to Odessa.

2. 16/11 ETA HKG to St. Petersburg

3. CT-900 unit weight (465G), extra weight (50G)

4. We will send 4 samples to you ASAP.

Best regards, Export Manager, Supplier Co., HK

4. HKTC Fax

To: CTC

Date: Oct. 25, 1991

How are you? I just came back from other meeting and know you need my fax return urgently.

Ref: HK to Odessa Nov. 11, 16

Vessel name: Mekhamik Bardetskiy V.25C W

Above is the shipment I have already booked and now we are waiting for their confirmation.

Ref: before we make appointment with SGS, please sign and return "The standard for telephone inspection":

Qty: 9000 pcs.

Type: CT-900 telephones

Major Defects:
1.   Dead
2.   Receiver does not function
3.   Microphone does not function
4.   Cannot dial
5.   Missing one or more dialing digits
6.   Ringer does not function
7.   No redialing function
8.   No mute function
9.   Wrong digit
10. Hook switch does not function
11. Cabinet damaged
12. Telephone cord missing or damaged

Minor defect:
1.   Telephone card loose/missing
2.   Buzzer weak
3.   Something inside cabinet
4.   Missing label
5.   Dirt stain on the cabinet
6.   Scratches on the cabinet

"If any defects are not covered in this standard, we will not consider these defects."

Awaiting your early reply.

B. regards, Export Manager, Supplier Co., HK

5. CTC Fax

To: Export Manager, Supplier Co., HK

From: CTC

Date: October 25, 1991

Re: S.G.S. Standards for Telephone Inspection

Ref: L/C No. 11616

Please find below the SGS standards for the inspection of our order of CT-900 telephones, quantity: 9,000 pcs, to be shipped from Hong Kong to Odessa November 11, 1991.

Major Defects

1. Dead.
2. Receiver does not function.
3. Microphone does not function.
4. Cannot dial.
5. Missing one or more dialing digits.
6. Ringer does not function.
7. No redialing function.
8. No mute function.
9. Wrong digit.
10. Hook switch does not function.
11. Cabinet damaged.
12. Telephone cord missing or damaged.
13. Telephone card loose/missing.
14. Something inside cabinet.
15. Dirt stain on the cabinet.

Minor Defects

1. Buzzer weak.
2. Missing label.
3. Minor scratches on the cabinet.

6. HKTC Fax

To: CTC

Date: Nov. 4, 1991

Ref: S.G.S. standards for telephone inspection

Dear Sirs:

Ref: L/C No. 11616

Please amend the S.G.S. standards for telephone inspection as following: (Ref. Your fax dated Oct. 25, 1991)

(a) In major defects part: No. 14 Something inside cabinet and No. 15 Dirt stain on the cabinet. These 2 points should belong to minor defects part.

(b) Please add in following sentence on S.G.S. standards telephone inspection as: "If any defects are not covered in the standard, we will not consider these defects."

After you read the above messages, please confirm and return to us immediately because the S.G.S. need it for inspection reference.

Awaiting your soonest reply.

B. rgds & tks, HKTC

P.S. (2) copy for your reference.

7. CTC reply to HKTC Nov. 4th Fax

To: HKTC

From: CTC Export Manager

Date: November 5, 1991

Re: S.G.S. Standards for Telephone Inspection

Thank you for your faxes and phone calls regarding amendments to the SGS standards and the exclusion clause for our shipment of telephones. I must tell you that we will not proceed with these amendments and that we are satisfied with the standards as they were presented to you in our fax of October 25. Please proceed with the inspection using the standards as they are.

I do apologize for the delay in getting back to you.

Best regards, CTC Export Manager

8. HKTC reply to CTC Fax

To: CTC

Date: Nov. 6, 1991

URGENT-URGENT

We just received your fax now, and we are very disappointed you do not amend the SGS standard. If you do not amend it to our fax then we are afraid we cannot meet SGS standard under your price because SGS standard is very tough, even your major items 14 and 15 are minor defects with international standard, but you gave the wrong instruction to SGS. You already instructed us to reduce price with additional metal weight and keep the same AQL condition as last shipment. How can we do it now?

We are waiting for your reply to start the production until you amend to our standard. If you would not like to change anything, the additional costing U.S. $0.20 is required on base price.

Please amend L/C soonest.

Awaiting for your early reply immed.

B. Rgds, Supplier, HK

9. CTC Fax

To: Supplier HK

From: CTC Export Manager

Date: November 6, 1991

Re: S.G.S. Standards for Telephone Inspection

Following our telecon of this morning, I agree to move major Standards 14 and 15 to the minor standards list. This should make the standards feasible. There should now be no problem for you to comply with our letter of credit and to provide us with quality products within the shipping date.

I am not incorporating the exclusion clause and our letter of credit will remain as it is, for you to comply with. We must be assured that you can manufacture quality products for the agreed price. As you know, this shipment is a trial order, an order that will determine if you will be the supplier of our future shipments. As of now, we have standing orders for five containers of telephones. We must be certain that you will comply with our contract as a reliable manufacturer.

I await the sample telephones that you promised to us two weeks ago. Please advise me of their arrival date.

I attached the revised SGS standards.

Regards, CTC Export Manager

10. The letter of credit issued by the Royal Bank of Canada to Overseas Trust Bank Ltd.

RECEIVING BANK NAME AND ADDRESS:	OVERSEAS TRUST BK LTD. HEAD OFFICE, OTB BUILDING 160 GLOUCESTER ROAD, GPO BOX 123 HONG KONG
DOCUMENT DELIVERED BY:	SWIFT

AS REQUESTED, WE ISSUE THE FOLLOWING DOCUMENTARY CREDIT:

FORM OF DOCUMENTARY CREDIT:	IRREVOCABLE
DOCUMENTARY CREDIT NUMBER:	11616
DATE OF ISSUE:	911023
DATE AND PLACE OF EXPIRY:	911226 HONG KONG
APPLICANT:	CTC
ADDRESS:	TORONTO, ONTARIO, CANADA
BENEFICIARY:	HKTC, SUPPLIER (FULL ADDRESS)
CURRENCY CODE, AMOUNT:	USD36,000.00
MAXIMUM CREDIT AMOUNT:	MAXIMUM
AVAILABLE WITH ... BY ...:	ANY BANK BY NEGOTIATION
DRAFTS AT:	DRAFT(S) AT SIGHT
DRAWEE:	DRAWN ON ROYAL BANK OF CANADA INTL. TRADE CENTRE - TORONTO, ONTARIO.
PARTIAL SHIPMENTS:	PROHIBITED
TRANSHIPMENT:	PERMITTED

LOADING ON BOARD/DISPATCH/TAKING IN CHARGE AT/FROM ... HONG KONG

FOR TRANSPORTATION TO ... ODESSA USSR

LATEST DATE OF SHIPMENT:	911120
CONTAINER SHIPMENT:	PERMITTED

SHIPMENT OF (GOODS): FASHION PHONES MODEL CT-900, USSR STANDARD, 60 VOLT, NET WEIGHT AT LEAST 515 GRAMS, LAST NUMBER REDIAL; 3,000 PCS. RED COLOUR, 3,000 PCS. BLACK COLOUR, 3,000 PCS. BLUE COLOUR - TOTAL 9,000 PCS WITH FLEXIBLE CORD 60CM (STRETCH 8 FT.) LONG COIL FROM PIN TO OTHER PIN.

COST, INSURANCE & FREIGHT

ODESSA USSR

DOCUMENTS REQUIRED:

- FULL SET CLEAN ON BOARD MARINE BILLS OF LADING SHOWING CANADIAN TRADING COMPANY AS SHIPPER CONSIGNED TO RUSSIAN BUYER (FULL ADDRESS) MARKED NOTIFY CONSIGNEE AND FREIGHT PREPAID.
- MARINE INSURANCE POLICY OR CERTIFICATE IN TRIPLICATE COVERING ALL RISKS AND WAR RISK INCLUDING INSTITUTE CARGO CLAUSE AND INSTITUTE STRIKE CLAUSE UNTIL WAREHOUSE DESTINATION FOR 110 PCT CIF VALUE IN NEGOTIABLE FORM WITH LOSS PAYABLE IN CANADA.
- COMMERCIAL INVOICE IN TRIPLICATE STATING THAT MARKS AND NUMBERS ARE ON BOXES/CRATES.
- PACKING LIST IN TRIPLICATE.
- CERTIFICATE OF ORIGIN IN TRIPLICATE.
- ORIGINAL SGS QUALITY AND QUANTITY INSPECTION CERTIFICATE AND THREE COPIES. THE QUALITY INSPECTION TO BE CONDUCTED ACCORDING TO THE STANDARD FOR INSPECTION OF CT9000 TELEPHONES (SEE SPECIFICATION OF INSPECTION ENCLOSED).
- BENEFICIARY CERTIFICATE STATING THAT ANY DOCUMENTS ATTACHED TO THE SHIPMENT DO NOT INDICATE THE VALUE OF GOODS.

ADDITIONAL CONDITIONS:

ADDITIONAL INSTRUCTIONS FOR PAYING/ACCEPTING/ NEGOTIATING BANK DOCUMENTS TO BE FORWARDED BY FEDERAL EXPRESS COURIER.

A DISCREPANCY FEE OF USD30.00 IS PAYABLE BY THE BENEFICI-
ARY FOR EACH DRAWING PRESENTED WHICH DOES NOT
STRICTLY COMPLY WITH THE TERMS OF THIS LETTER OF
CREDIT AND WHICH HAS TO BE REFERRED TO THE APPLI-
CANT.

CHARGES: ALL BANK CHARGES OUTSIDE CANADA ARE
              FOR BENEFICIARY'S ACCOUNT.

PERIOD FOR PRESENTATION: DOCUMENTS MUST BE
                          PRESENTED WITHIN 15 DAYS
                          AFTER DATE OF TRANSPORT
                          DOCUMENTS BUT BEFORE
                          EXPIRY DATE OF CREDIT.

CONFIRMATION INSTRUCTIONS: WITHOUT.

INSTRUCTIONS FOR PAYING/ACCEPTING/NEGOTIATING
BANK.

UNLESS OTHERWISE SPECIFIED NEGOTIATING BANK WILL
FORWARD ALL DRAFT(S) AND DOCUMENTS TO US IN ONE
MAILING.

ADVISE THROUGH BANK YR FO TAN BRANCH

THIS CREDIT IS SUBJECT TO THE UNIFORM CUSTOMS AND
PRACTICE FOR DOCUMENTARY CREDITS 1983 REVISION, I.C.C.,
PUBLICATION NUMBER 400.

ROYAL BANK OF CANADA

AUTHORIZED SIGNATURE   OTHER SIGNATURE

11. HKTC Fax stating the finding of the SGS Report and asking for acceptance of quality problems

To: CTC

From: HKTC

Date: November 13, 1991

Re: samples – We have sent two samples to you last week. If you have not received it within two days, we will send other two samples to you again.

Re: shipment – The shipping co. has confirmed the shipment date and 9,000 pcs. CT-900 will be shipped to you this 15/11/91.

S.G.S. Hong Kong Ltd. has finished checking and all of the goods passed their AQL 2.5/4.0 (major/minor) accept No. 10/14. But they need us to inform you to accept the following five remark points which were copied from S.G.S. text. Otherwise they cannot issue certificate, only issue a report with those remarks.

(a) SGS text: No digital scale was available for weight measurement during inspection.
Maker explanation: we have used digital scale to weigh our product on samples in Hong Kong office and the weight is over 515G/per unit. Even in production, our worker used mechanical scale on each unit and each unit was over 515G. Digital scale is not useful in manufacture.

(b) SGS text: Some inspected samples found silk screen printing on dialing key unclear which were similar to your reference samples.
Maker explanation: silk-screen printing on dialing key is same as samples we sent to you before you placed order.

(c) SGS text: Some inspected samples found dialing key will rub against keyboard panel when pressed, causing keys to slightly jam.
Maker explanation: This problem is caused by the plastic molding, because it is an old tooling, but it has not affected the telephone dialing function. Please give us instruction.

(d) SGS text: All inspected samples found mold marks on the top edge of handset cabinet.
Maker explanation: Problem caused by molding because it is old.

(e) SGS text: No carton numbers marked on export cartons during our inspection.
Maker explanation: usually, for the container loading we do not write the carton number on each carton. If you need, we can write it on.

After you read above messages, please confirm and return to us immed. Because the SGS need it to issue the certificate.

We look forward to hearing from you soonest. B. Rgds., HKTC

12. CTC Fax cancelling the order due to quality problems:

To: Export Manager

From: Buyer Co.

Date: Nov. 14, 1991

Following a telecon this morning with the President and Vice President of our company, I am instructed to tell you that we will not accept the telephones in their present state. We are concerned about the jamming of the keys, the mould marks on the body of the phone, and the smudging of the print on the keys. We will not send shoddy telephones to the USSR.

We will extend our L/C if you can arrange for these defects to be corrected, and for the weight to be checked digitally. Please advise immediately how this is possible and the next shipping date to Odessa.

We await your news.

With regards, Export Manager, CTC

13. Supplier arguments for acceptance of the phones, "A lesson in negotiating skills"

To: CTC

Attn: Export Manager

Date: Nov. 15, 1991

Your instruction we just received today and we study with our Engineer Dept. Manager and he explained as:

1. Key slightly jammed
This point is very minor on low-end products and even those points did not affect telephone dialing function.

2. Mould marks on the body
This point is very minor on low-end products. Because this minor point did not cause telephone malfunction, and any plastic must have this mark on in-section. If no mark, how was the cabinet made?

3. Silk-screen printing
This point is very minor on low-end products, this silk-screen printing is same as on the sample we gave you before you placed order, and also this minor point did not cause telephone malfunction. Because it was round button, silk screen must be hand-made, cannot use machine.

4. Digital scale for weighing
We cannot export a digital scale to China from Hong Kong because we do not have export contract. But we have weighed working sample and extra metal weighed (101 x 44 x 0.33 MM) 50G In Hong Kong by digital scale before we started our production. Also, during our production, we used a mechanical scale to weigh each unit. If you are still concerned on this point, we can issue a certificate to certify each of the unit weights is at least 515G.

By above explanation, please accept those points because our product has passed S.G.S. AQL 2.5/4.0 (major/minor) which you required. But if you need us to correct those points we think it is very difficult.

(1) We need to have another new mould.

(2) We must buy another key button with silk-screen, with original in-section form tooling, but it is very expensive. It costs US$0.20 each.

We look forward to hearing from you soonest.

Regards, HKTC

14. Reply from the Moscow office of the Canadian Trading Co. stating that the client has refused to renew his L/C to Canadian Trading Co. and, therefore, Canadian Trading Co. is unable to renew its L/C to the supplier

To: Supplier Co., HK

From: Moscow Representative, Canadian Trading Co.

Date: Nov. 26, 1991

Thank you for your fax yesterday. Due to the bad report of the SGS and the delay of shipment, our customer has refused to renew his L/C to us. However, he has asked us to wait four weeks, giving us hope for the renewal of this and other orders. Therefore, we have no other alternative but to ask you to wait.

We are sorry to inform you of this outcome and we value our relationship with you.

Sincerely, Moscow Representative of Canadian Trading Co.

P.S. Please feel free to move our order to another client. We look forward to doing business with you in the future and we hope this deal will not damage our affiliation.

15. Supplier final arguments for amendments to extend the latest shipment dated of the L/C and accept the quality as is for the phones

To: Canadian Trading Co.

Date: Nov. 26, 1991

Ref.   9000 sets Model CT-900 Shipment Schedule

We would like to inform you that this shipment time is on Nov. 30, 1991. Please confirm this shipment as soon as you can. Because since Dec. 1st, 91, the freight will be increased US$300.00 per 20F shipment from Hong Kong to Odessa.

We look forward to hearing from you soonest.

B. Rgds, Supplier Co., HK

16. HKTC's closing arguments

To: Canadian Trading Co.

Attn: Moscow Representative

Date: Nov. 27, 1991

Ref: 9000 pcs. Of CT-900 Cancelling

Thank you for your fax just received an hour ago.

We are very sorry to hear that you have cancelled this order. It is a big problem for us.

This product, with weight and 8Ft. coil cord, we have specially made for you to your requirements. Unfortunately, we cannot sell the goods to others, they cannot accept high price with weight and extra length cord (your price is special price never quoted for others). Now we would like you to understand our situation; manufacturer needs the buyer L/C confirmed and then starts the production for buyer; if any client who opens a L/C to confirm order and then finally cancels it, we think all of the manufacturers will be bankrupt. It is very easy for you to say that "This order will be cancelled, sorry!" But for us, it is a big problem.

We are waiting for you to advise your buyer to amend the L/C and accept this order. Frankly, the goods function is very good, and has passed SGS serious inspection.

We look forward to hearing from you soonest.

Conclusion

In business a win-win situation is the best outcome. But in this case all parties lost. The Russian buyer did not receive the shipment of phones ordered from the Canadian Trading Co. The latter did not enjoy the U.S. $9,000 gross profit but instead incurred L/C charges of about $500 Canadian dollars and long distance tel/fax charges of about $600 between Russia, Canada, and Hong Kong; and the Hong Kong supplier got stuck with 9,000 phones.

The supplier ended up in a bad position, but the consequences of 9,000 phones of poor quality arriving in Russia would have been worse. The SGS Quality Certificate was able to prevent a possible disaster. It is important to note that if a credit were to simply call for an "SGS quality certificate," documentarily a bank could accept an

SGS certificate with a notation that the product is of poor quality, because the L/C did not spell out the criteria under which an inspection should have been performed. It is therefore important for the buyer to spell out the criteria required for inspection inside the text of the L/C. The lessons from this case study are self-explanatory. The letter of credit is designed to protect both the buyer and the seller, but depending on the terms and conditions of a particular credit, one side may benefit more than the other.

CASE STUDY #2
Performance Bond - The Vessel Named "Yick Fat"

How to protect yourself against unscrupulous buyers and unforeseen events.

This case study is based on a real contract between a steel trading company (STC) and a Korean steel mill (KSM) on the purchase of 15,000/mt of billets produced by a Russian Iron & Steel Works and shipped through the Black Sea port of Novorossiysk to Pohang, Korea.

Reproduced below are the contract, letter of credit, performance bond, and correspondence between the steel trading company, the agent representing the Korean mill, and the freight broker. The contract between the Russian producer and the steel trading company is purposely omitted in this casestudy for the purpose of simplicity.

1) Contract

Contract No. JK2607.1   Ma 17 31, 1994

Buyer: Korean Steel Mill (KSM)
                Address , South Korea

This is to confirm that KSM (as "Buyer") purchase from STC (as "Seller") and the Seller's sale to the Buyer, of the goods described herein subject to the following terms and conditions:

Description: Hot Rolled Steel Billets

Quality: Technical conditions / Size detail as per schedule "A" attached hereto.

Quantity: Shipment of 15,000 mt (+/- 10% at Seller's Option) from Novorossiysk, Black Sea Port.

Price: US$243.00 per mt CNF FO COD Pohang port South Korea.

Total Amount: US$3,648,000.00 (+/- 10%)

Payment: Letter of Credit

Shipment: Shipment to be made before July 30, 1994

Manufacturer: Buyer's care.

Loading port: 15,000 (+/- 10%) MI of the steel billets will be loaded at Port of Novorossiysk, Black Sea Port.

Letter of Credit: Royal Bank of Canada, 180 Wellington St. W., Toronto, Ontario, Canada M5J 1J1 Telex: 06-22231

The buyer shall open an irrevocable letter of credit via cable, payable at sight, at the counter of negotiating bank before June 10, 1994 after signing of the contract in favour of STC (full address, tel/fax/telex).

Instructions to advising bank: Please add your confirmation if requested by beneficiary. It is understood that confirmation charges will be at the A/C of beneficiary.

L/C to be payable against organization of following documents:

(a) commercial invoice in triplicate.

(b) 3/3 full set of clean on board ocean bill of lading, marked "Freight Prepaid" made out to order of the issuing bank.

(c) fax or copy of the Quality Certificate issued by the Mill or authorized organization. (Originals to be sent by courier no later than 10 days after B/L date).

(d) beneficiary's packing list.

L/C must allow for:

• Plus/minus 10 per cent on total quantity and L/C amount acceptable

• Charter party B/L acceptable

• B/L issued in Canada acceptable

• Third party shipper and documents acceptable

• L/C is freely negotiable with the Royal Bank of Canada

• B/L claused "material atmospheric rusted, unprotected" or similar clause acceptable

• Partial shipment allowed

• Transhipment not allowed

- Latest shipment date July 10, 1994

- Expiry date: August 21, 1994 at the counter of the advising/negotiating bank in Toronto

- Presentation of documents within 21 days after on board date, but within the validity of credit

- L/C payable at beneficiary's bank counter in Toronto in U.S. dollars with T/T reimbursement on a first class New York Bank

- All documents can be issued in English or Russian with English translation

Weight bases: To be based on actual draft survey by SGS at discharge port against B/L weight with zero point five (0.5) per cent franchise deductible, Buyer must send SGS surveyor's survey report at discharge port irrespective of whether there is short weight or not.

Discharge terms: The cargo to be discharged at the rate of 3,000 mt per WWDSHEX UU, if used, actual working time to count laytime for discharging shall commence at 1 p.m. if notice of readiness is given before noon and at 8 a.m. next working day if notice of readiness is given after noon.

Time actually used before commencement of laytime shall count, time waiting for berth to count as laytime.

If the vessel has arrived at or off the discharge port and in all respect ready for discharging of cargo, master can/may tender notice of readiness in writing or by cable/telex, WIPON, WIBON, WCCON, WFPON.

Demurrage/Dispatch: COD/CQD

ORIGINAL TERMS AND CONDITIONS

1. ENTIRE AGREEMENT: Unless otherwise agreed in writing by the Buyer, these terms and conditions supersede any earlier terms and conditions and shall override any other terms and conditions stipulated by the Seller in any other documents or in negotiations.

2. IMPORT LICENCE, ETC: The Buyer will take the necessary steps to obtain import licences and/or exchange permits of the country stated under "Destination" on the face hereof (the "Destination").

Moreover, the Buyer shall not be responsible for any failure or delay in performance in regard to the foregoing if caused by any reasons whatsoever beyond its control including, but not limited to, restrictions on import or payments imposed by the government of the Destination or the government of Canada or relative exchange bank subsequent to the execution of this contract.

3. LETTER OF CREDIT: Before June 10, 1994 after acceptance of this Contract by Seller, Buyer shall open an irrevocable, transferable, confirmable Letter of Credit via cable, payable at sight, at the counter of negotiating bank.

4. CHARGER, ETC: All taxes, fees, other charges, and surcharges incurred in the country of shipment and/or origin on the merchandise and/or containers and/or documents including the certificate of origin shall be the responsibility of the Seller and for the Seller's account and the merchandise shall be carried, by the usual route or routes and modes of conveyance of a type normally used for the transport of the merchandise described in this contract.

Bill of Lading date shall be proof of date of shipment in the absence of evidence to the contrary. Notice of particulars of shipment shall be sent by the Seller to the Buyer so that the Buyer shall receive the same within 7 days after shipment.

5. WARRANTY: The Seller warrants that the Seller shall be responsible for any failure to supply the commodity in terms of the contract, provided that the failure is due to the actual fault or negligence of the Seller. It is accepted by the purchaser that the Seller is entitled to rely on the specifications and declarations of quality given by the Manufacturer or Supplier of the commodity and that the Seller is not liable for any loss suffered by the Buyer as a result of the Seller relying on the accuracy of the specification and declaration of quality given by the manufacturer or supplier of the commodity.

6. FORCE MAJEURE: In case of an event such as strikes, lockouts, lack of transportation facilities, fraudulent acts, or breaches of contract by third parties and any other matter beyond the control of the Seller or Buyer preventing the Seller from delivering or making available the commodity, this contract shall be suspended but If the contract is suspended for more than 3 calendar months, the Buyer or Seller shall have the option of canceling the contract, provided that any such notice of cancellation is in writing.

7. CLAIMS: Should any defects in the goods delivered be found, or should the goods not be in conformity with the technical condition stipulated in the contract, or should any shortage in the weight of the goods be found, the Buyer has the right to submit a claim to the Seller - on cargo value only - in writing which must be received by Seller within 30 days after arrival of vessel together with the survey report issued by SGS surveyor with detailed tally report and original short landed memo issued and sighted by master and/or vessel's agent.

8. RESERVATION OF TITLE: Until payment in full has been made to Seller, the goods shall remain the property of the Seller, but the risk thereof and all liability to third parties in respect thereof shall pass to the Buyer on passing ship's rail. Should the goods be processed or mixed with any goods then the new articles produced shall become the property of the seller either solely or, if the goods are owned by any other party, jointly with that party.

9. ARBITRATION: Any dispute or difference arising out of or relating to this contract, or the breach thereof which cannot be settled amicably without undue delay by the interested parties shall be settled by arbitration pursuant to The Arbitration Act of Province of Ontario. The award shall be final and binding upon both parties.

10. GOVERNING LAW: This contract shall be governed by and construed under the Laws of the Province of Ontario.

11. Remark: Fax contract is operative.

12. PERFORMANCE BOND: The Seller will issue Performance Bond equal to two per cent (2%) of contract value in favour of the Buyer in order to activate the Buyer's L/C. The Buyer accepts that the performance bond will guarantee only the quality of steel billets as per chemical specifications mentioned in the contract No. JK2607.1.

Remark: 30 days nego hold.

Buyer: KOREAN STEEL MILL (KSM).

Seller: STEEL TRADING COMPANY (STC)

Authorized Officer   Authorized Officer

May 31, 1994

SCHEDULE A FORMS AN INTEGRAL PART OF THE PURCHASE AND SALE CONTRACT BETWEEN STC (AS SELLER) AND KSM (AS BUYER) IN CONTRACT NO. JK 2607.1

Commodity: Hot Rolled Steel Billets

Size: 120 x 120 x 11700 mm (+/0 200mm)

Quantity: 15,000 mt in one lot (+/- 10%)

Chemical Specifications: C: 0.25 - 0.29%
                            Mn: 1.20 - 1.50%
                            Si: 0.15 - 0.55%
                            P: 0.045% Max.
                            S: 0.050% Max.

2. Performance Bond issued by Supplier, the Steel Trading Company (STC), to the Korean Steel Mill (KSM) Buyer

DATE: JULY 4, 1994

TO: ROYAL BANK OF CANADA
         SEOUL, KOREA

TEST: 0076315
         TEST ON USD 72,900.00

PLEASE ADVISE KSM THAT WE ISSUED IN THEIR FAVOUR OUR IRREVOCABLE STANDBY LETTER OF CREDIT NO. P71393T06702 AS FOLLOWS:

QUOTE

BENEFICIARY: KSM (FULL ADDRESS)
                SOUTH KOREA

BY ORDER OF: STC (FULL ADDRESS)
                ONTARIO, CANADA

AMOUNT: USD72,900.00 (SEVENTY TWO THOUSAND
                NINE HUNDRED UNITED STATES DOLLARS)

EXPIRY DATE: AUGUST 31, 1994 AT OUR COUNTERS IN TORONTO, ONTARIO

WE HEREBY ISSUE IN YOUR FAVOUR THIS IRREVOCABLE STANDBY LETTER OF CREDIT WHICH IS AVAILABLE BY PAYMENT AGAINST YOUR WRITTEN DEMAND ADDRESSED TO ROYAL BANK OF CANADA, INTERNATIONAL TRADE CENTRE - ONTARIO, 180 WELLINGTON STREET WEST, TORONTO, ONTARIO BEARING THE CLAUSE QUOTE DRAWN UNDER STANDBY LETTER OF CREDIT NO. P71393T06702 ISSUED BY ROYAL BANK OF CANADA, INTERNATIONAL TRADE CENTRE - ONTARIO, 180 WELLINGTON STREET WEST, TORONTO, ONTARIO, UNQUOTE, WHEN ACCOMPANIED BY THE FOLLOWING DOCUMENTS:

1. BENEFICIARY'S SIGNED CERTIFICATE SPECIFYING AMOUNT CLAIMED AND STATING THAT THE AMOUNT DRAWN REPRESENTS TWO PER CENT OF L/C NO. M0633406NS00107 FOR USD3,645,000.00 ISSUED BY KOREA EXCHANGE BANK, SEOUL, KOREA AND STC HAS FAILED TO SHIP THE GOODS DESCRIBED IN L/C NO. M0633406NS00107.

2. A CERTIFICATE ISSUED BY SGS STATING THAT THE GOODS DESCRIBED IN L/C NO. M0633406NS00107 ARE NOT IN ACCORDANCE WITH THE SPECIFICATION UNDER CONTRACT NO. JK 2607.1.

PARTIAL DRAWINGS ARE NOT PERMITTED.

SPECIAL CONDITIONS: THIS STANDBY LETTER OF CREDIT WILL BECOME OPERATIVE ONLY UPON RECEIPT BY US OF AN AMENDMENT EXTENDING SHIPPING DATE TO JULY 30, 1994 OR LATER UNDER L/C NO. M0633406NS00107. WE UNDERTAKE TO ADVISE YOU BY WAY OF AN AMENDMENT WHEN THIS STANDBY LETTER OF CREDIT BECOMES OPERATIVE.

EXCEPT OTHERWISE EXPRESSLY STATED THIS CREDIT ISSUED SUBJECT TO UNIFORM CUSTOMS AND PRACTICE FOR DOCUMENTARY CREDITS, 1993 REVISION, ICC PUBLICATION NO.500.

WE ENGAGE TO HONOUR PRESENTATIONS SUBMITTED WITHIN THE TERMS AND CONDITIONS INDICATED ABOVE STOP UNQUOTE.

THIS TELEX IS CONSIDERED THE OPERATIVE INSTRUMENT
STOP.

MANAGER CUSTOMER SERVICES
LETTER OF CREDIT/GUARANTEES
INTERNATIONAL TRADE CENTRE - ONTARIO
(SIGNED) ROYAL BANK OF CANADA

TO: RECEIVING BANK NAME AND ADDRESS
      0076315
      ROYAL BANK
      KYOBO BUILDING, 7TH FLOOR
      1-1, 1-KA, CHONGRO, CHONGRO-KU
      PO 5374, SEOUL, KOREA

DOCUMENT DELIVERED BY: CABLE

ADVISE BENEFICIARY WE AMEND DOCUMENTARY CREDITS AS
FOLLOWS:

SENDING BANK'S REFERENCE

RECEIVING BANK'S REFERENCE

NONREF

DATE OF ISSUE: 940704

BENEFICIARY: KSM
               (FULL ADDRESS), SOUTH KOREA

NARRATIVE

THIS STANDBY LETTER OF CREDIT IS CONSIDERED OPERATIVE.

ALL OTHER TERMS AND CONDITIONS REMAIN UNCHANGED.

BANK TO BANK INFORMATION

THIS TELEX IS CONSIDERED THE OPERATIVE INSTRUMENT.

Following the issuance of the performance bond guaranteeing delivery of the steel products specified under contract No. JK2607.1 and the issuance of letter of credit by the buyer, an unforeseen situation occurred. This situation is described in detail through reproduction of actual fax correspondence between the freight broker (FB), the agent for the Korean Steel Mill (Agent), the buyer (KSM), and the supplier (STC).

3. Fax from the freight broker advising the charter party, STM, of the occurrence:

Gentlemen Good Morning

Re: M.V. Yick Fat - Novorssiysk/Pohang

As per advice received from master of evening August the 1st. Whilst loading part cargo carelessness of shore stevedore caused two 6/8 mt billets to be dropped from above the ships hold onto its tank tops at the bottom of the hold. The two billets fell approximately 55/60 ft on to the tank tops puncturing the steel deck and entered in the fuel oil tanks immediately below. This resulted in two large holes, damage to the fuel oil heating coils, and distortion to the vesse's immediate main frames.

All loading had to be ceased till Lloyd's official surveyors arrived and inspected. All fuel oil tanks had to be flooded to ensure interest gases removed.

Due to the severe nature of the damage and the position of the holes, Lloyds have insisted that permanent repairs and not temporary repairs have to be made before the vessel is allowed to sail.

Vessel has had to move off the berth to effect repairs and will have to wait till same are completed and surveyors give their official approval that they meet all classification specifications. Prior to surveyors giving such approval all the damaged area and repairs and welding have to be x-rayed.

Once vessel has been officially cleared she has to finish final loading part cargo. As of today the expected time of sailing from Novorssiysk is between the 12th and 14th of August as per earlier vessel will sail directly to Kosichang-Haikou-Fangeng and Pohang.

4. Agent for KSM informs the STC of order cancellation:

From: Agent for Buyer

To: STC

Date: Aug. 12, 1994

Ref: 940812-3

Re: Billet 15000mt

Tks for your kind attention in advance.

We are very regretful to inform you that this order was cancelled by KSM due to late shipment/departure from loading port.

Actually, your cargo-late arrival is making a lot of serious problem/damage to KSM's production schedule. In the meantime, KSM placed substitute-order with Turkey in order to cope with emergency caused by your late shipment. This cargo will be arrived at Pohang, Korea between middle of September - end of September.

Please be advised that your shipment was not executed within latest shipping date which was already amended according to your request and KSM is not in a position to extend latest shipping date any longer due to above situation. So your order was cancelled automatically and P-Bond will be drawn by KSM as non-performance penalty.

Your kind understanding would be appreciated.

Encl: Official letter from KSM

B. Regards, Agent (Signature)

(Additional Remarks in manuscript): This cancellation is totally beyond our control. Because of this matter the relationship between our company (Agent) and KSM became the worst. So our future business with KSM will be entirely jeopardized.

5. Reply to Fax Ref: 940812-3 from the STC:

To: KSM (cc: Agent for KSM)

From: President, STC

Date: August 15, 1994

Re: Contract No. JK2607.1

TOP URGENT

We understand your inconvenience with this first shipment, and we are in the same difficult situation since we (STC) have prepaid the Russian Steel Mill (producer) for this 15,000 MT steel billets, paid transportation cost from the mill to the port, and committed to the owners of M.V. "Yick Fat." Our staff made many trips to Volgograd to convince the mill to accept your order of high Mn content and size 11.7 M. In the end, we produced the quality and size as per contract with you and we have brought all goods to port of Novorossiysk in a designated time.

The fact is that there was an accident on the vessel "Yick Fat," which was "beyond the control of the Seller or Buyer," see General Terms and Conditions point 8 Force Majeure Contract No. JK 2607.1.

Even if the Force Majeure did not use this wording, we, as partners and people who want to work long-term with each other, should look for a way out of this situation together.

Nevertheless, repairs are concluded, the vessel is scheduled to depart by August 25, 1994, and the SGS Quality Certificate is in accordance with the L/C.

Again, this delay is due to a Force Majeure situation, and not the fault of our company.

I urge you to think over the situation and come to a mutual agreement for all sides, noting our Contract No. JK2607.1 point 8 Force Majeure, "... the contract shall be suspended but if the contract is suspended for more than 3 calender months, the buyer or seller shall have the option of cancelling the contract, providing that any such notice of cancellation is in writing."

Therefore, I submit to you that KSM cannot legally cancel the contract before 3 calendar months from the Latest Shipment Date have expired. Your company should amend the L/C if the Force Majeure situation is resolved before this 3 month suspension period, as per contract.

Please we ask you kindly to amend the L/C Latest Shipment Date to August 30, 1994 and the Expiry Date accordingly.

Please find enclosed a letter from M.V. "Yick Fat" agents, FB confirming the current situation.

Awaiting your swift reply. With great respect, President, STC

6. Fax reply from the agent for KSM

To: STC

Date: Aug. 22, 1994

Ref. No.: 940822-4

Re: Billets 15,000 mt

According to reliable sources, KSM was already dishonoured last week and will be bankrupted in the coming year.

So, we can understand KSM has fallen into a really difficult condition. Under above circumstances, it is impossible for KSM to accept your material at all.

You have no choice but to divert your material to another customer. You are kindly requested not to ship your material by "Yick Fat" this time and wait until the contract with the other customer is completed as we are trying to find other customers.

And also please do not present shipping document for negotiation with your bank based on related L/C which issued by KSM.

Rgds, Agent for KSM

7. Defensive action by STC - Fax addressed to the Royal Bank regarding the performance bond:

To: Royal Bank of Canada

From: STC

Date: August 15, 1994

Re: Our L/C P71393T06702

Dear Sirs:

Regarding our P71393T06702-06702 Beneficiary: KSM

Please be informed and keep on file that we have presented an SGS Certificate of Quality in accordance with the letter of credit E70670T02126.

Therefore, our Performance Bond (PB) should not be drawn prior to expiry. All has gone well.

Thank you for your help.

With great respect, STC

8. Reprinted below an actual telex message sent by the Korean bank on behalf of the KSM cancelling the letter of credit:

!!! LIVE !!! LIVE !!! LIVE !!! LIVE !!! LIVE !!! LIVE !!! LIVE !!!

Req by: TOR AUTOLCT   In: AUT PRT 08/23/94   07:10

ICN: CA 940823-001875-000 Que: CA TOR LCT ADMR PRI 150

Msg Type: RECEIVED   Poss Dup: N Pri: N

Time Created: 08/23/94 03:27

Correspondent: 0047654   II

Name: KOREA EXCHANGE BK., SEOUL

Owner Office: TOR/LCT

Address: FOREIGN BUSINESS DEPT.

Address: I.P.O. BOX 2924

City: SEOUL   Country: KOREA   PC:

Parent ICN: ca 940823-001875-000

Input Test: N Swift OSN: F940823KOEX

Service: SWF Ref: F940823ROYCCAT22XXX Sequence: 910

Test Result: TESTED

TO: ROYCCAT22XXX   ROYAL BANK OF CANADA TOR(T22)

FROM: KOEXERSEXXX   KOREA EXCHANGE BK.,
                      SEOUL (KOREA)

CIF NUMBER: 0047654   TYPE II UID:

MSG TYPE: 707 AMENDMENT TO A DOCUMENTARY CREDIT

20 /   SENDER'S REFERENCE: M0633406NS00107

21 /   RECEIVER'S REFERENCE: NONREF

31C/   DATE OF ISSUE: 94/06/14

30 /   DATE OF AMENDMENT: 94/08/23

59 /   BENEFICIARY: STC

79 /   NARRATIVE:

THIS CREDIT IS TO BE CANCELLED SUBJECT TO THE CONSENT OF THE BENEFICIARY

PLS CABLE ADVISE US CANCELLATION EFFECTED

Note: the beneficiary did not agree to such cancellation, but could not use the L/C in any case because the time for shipment had expired.

144

Conclusion

The steel trading company was able to avoid the drawing of U.S. $72,900, the Performance Bond amount, by wording the text of the PB guarantee in a way that prevented the Korean Steel Mill, Beneficiary under the PB, from collecting. To be successful in drawing under the given PB the Korean Steel Mill had to present the following documents:

1. Beneficiary's signed certificate specifying amount claimed and stating that the amount drawn represents two per cent of L/C No. M0633406NS00107 for USD3,645,000.00 issued by Korea Exchange Bank, Seoul, Korea and that STC has failed to ship the goods described in L/C No. M0633406NS00107.

2. A certificate issued by SGS stating that the goods described in L/C No. M0633406NS00107 are not in accordance with the specification under Contract No. JK 2607.1.

By accepting an SGS certificate as one of the documents needed for drawing under the PB, the Korean Steel Mill made a mistake for the following reasons:

- KSM accepted a third party document that it did not control since the supplier - STC - paid for the SGS inspection at loading port. Hence SGS would deliver the certificate to the party that contracted SGS to perform the inspection service, in this case, the supplier.

- KSM accepted that if SGS found the goods in accordance with the specification under Contract No. JK2607.1, it would not have a basis for a claim. The Performance Bond's original purpose was to protect the buyer against late delivery. However, KSM accepted a document in the PB dealing with quality of the steel product and not the delivery of the product on time. Providing that the supplier delivered the steel in the size and chemistry as contracted but not on time, the buyer would not be able to draw on the PB even if it had the original SGS certificate.

The impression that the KSM acted in an uninformed or unprofessional manner is false. On the contrary, the quality of the steel supplied under the contract was very important to the Koreans, especially due to the high manganese content of the steel billets. The KSM wanted an SGS report to show the Mn (manganese) content of 1.20-1.50 per cent in accordance with the contract. Therefore, the SGS quality of certificate was also part of the PB. The ideal situation for the KSM would have been to order SGS quality inspection at their expense and present it under the letter of credit.

The buyer accepted the wording of the PB as presented by the supplier assuming that all would go well. In most instances where the buyer trusts the supplier's ability to deliver the goods in accordance with a signed contract, there is no need for a Performance Bond. In this case, however, all did not go as planned. KSM went bankrupt and could not extend the validity of the letter of credit. If KSM had extended the latest shipment date and the expiry of the L/C, the supplier would have delivered the billets on MV "Yick Fat." It was not the fault of the supplier that an accident happened. On the contrary, the supplier did everything possible to repair the vessel as quickly as possible to resume loading. It was the buyer in the end who acted in an unscrupulous manner and tried to collect under the PB. KSM was not successful in drawing the PB and STC was forced to resell the 15,000/mt billets to another client, losing US$20 per mt as a contingency of the distress sale. The funds secured under the PB, US$72,900, were saved. If the PB had been worded in a way wherein the buyer simply had to present a receipt of non-performance, the PB would have been drawn upon, and STC would have been out US$72,900.

CASE STUDY #3

Exclusive Rights - "How to Get Them, How to Protect Them"

In 1989 a Canadian Trading Company (CTC) approached a Belgian producer of brick-making equipment (BP) with an enquiry for a small brick-making plant for the Moscow region in Russia. Prior to 1989 BP had never sold any brick-making equipment to Russia or any other of the former USSR countries. BP did, however, have experience in exporting products to African countries and the Middle East. When CTC asked for exclusive rights to all of the Soviet Union, BP was cautious, but felt it had nothing to lose because it did not expect that there would be very much demand for its products due to the cold climate and the non-convertibility of the local currency (ruble). CTC pressed for an exclusive rights agreement, and BP signed a short, conditional agreement based on a minimum quantity of brick-making machines to be sold in the USSR market per year.

BP's president was pleasantly surprised when instead of ten machines (minimum requirement under the agreement), CTC sold over one hundred machines in the first year. Soon clients from Moscow, Kiev, Baku, Tbilisi, and other ex-Soviet cities started to approach BP directly at its head office in Belgium asking for brick-making machines for export.

At first BP advised prospective clients to contact its exclusive representative, CTC, but later it became difficult to monitor which orders were for the USSR and which orders were for other markets. Many clients wanting to go around CTC's back approached BP through third countries such as Poland, Czechoslovakia, and Hungary. Other traders from Western Europe, USA, and Canada also entered the market as they too had buyers in Russia, Ukraine, or other republics who wanted to purchase BP machines but not through CTC. In 1991 BP received from five to ten calls or faxes daily asking for the USSR specification CERAMATIC/CERADES package.

"Ceramatic" dry press brick-making machine and "Cerades" disintegrator

It all came down to economics. The BP factory price was U.S. $45,000-50,000. CTC's Russian price was U.S. $55,000-60,000.

Obviously other traders could not make as large a profit by buying through CTC and wanted to buy direct, despite the fact that CTC offered traders commissions of $5,000 per unit on sales to their USSR clients.

On one occasion BP even received a wire transfer of US$1 million from one trader wanting to buy for the Russian market. The transfer was made cash in advance without a prior invoice or contract. The trader wanted to buy only from BP direct.

What about the exclusive rights agreement with CTC? Should BP have refused a US$1 million sale and told the buyer to deal with CTC? Despite the exclusivity agreement, BP did sell directly to that trader, but paid CTC a 10 per cent commission on the sale. Many other sales were also made by BP to other traders for the USSR market despite the clear obligations of exclusivity to CTC.

Sometimes a commission was paid on these sales, other times BP claimed that orders were destined for Poland or other East European countries for which CTC had no exclusive rights. Only through close monitoring of USSR borders was CTC able to keep track of BP machines imported into its "exclusive" market. Where CTC had proof of third party sales into its market, a commission was paid, no questions asked.

It is important to note that despite other traders intervening into the relationship between BP and CTC, CTC was able to maintain its exclusive rights through consistently making block orders of ten to twenty machines at a time. As CTC was still the largest buyer of BP machines, the producer was happy to maintain the relationship.

Could have CTC have taken BP to court for breaking the agreement? The answer is "yes," in theory, but in practice, it would not have been a smart move. Both companies worked towards the same goal, penetration of the USSR market, and both were successful through cooperation with each other.

The Big Bluff: Big Brick-making Plants.

One of the factors that kept BP loyal or almost loyal to its exclusive distributor was a project to develop sales in USSR; a 35 million brick-per-year modern brickworks (project cost, U.S. $12 to14 million). CTC located a local producer of kilns in Moscow, which could be subcontracted for such a project. The local producer helped to reduce the project cost by $800,000 and would help make the BP project more competitive against German, Spanish, and French producers of similar equipment.

By 1993 when the project for this large brickworks moved from the drawing board into a commercial proposal, the financial situation in Russia and the surrounding republics had changed dramatically. Inflation dried up ruble capital, and where previously in 1990-91 various sectors of USSR economy had government "budget" money (which did not belong to anybody), in 1993-94, market forces and privatization made it more difficult for traders to sell large projects. By 1993 new orders for small brickmaking plants dried up for two reasons. The first was inflation; the second was that seven local Russian factories had begun production of similar equipment, circumventing the BP patent. It made no sense to challenge the local producers through the courts since such action would not yield any results. Nevertheless the overall goal of keeping BP faithful to CTC was served. The Belgian producer, hopeful of selling a few large projects in Russia and Ukraine, continued to pay commissions to CTC on sales made through third party traders into Russia.

AGENCY AGREEMENT between the Belgian Producer and Canadian Trading Company is reprinted below:

An agreement made this Wednesday the 16th of August nineteen hundred eighty nine, etween Belgian Producer of Brick Making Equipment (BP) (hereinafter referred to as "the Company") of one part and Canadian Trading Company (CTC) (herein referred to as "the Agent" of the other part.)

Hereby it is agreed as follows:

Article 1: territory

The "Territory" means USSR

Article 2: products

the "Products" means the current and future products from the dry pressing range offered for sale buy the Company.

• CERAMATIC (automatic press) of any type with moulds and spare parts.

• CERAMAN (manual press) of any type with moulds and spare parts.

• CERADES (disintegrator) of any type with spare parts.

Article 3: products modifications/withdrawal

In view of possible changes in technological or business conditions, it is expressly understood and agreed that the Company reserves the right to modify specifications or withdraw any produces from sale without incurring any liability or financial compensation towards the Agent.

Article 4: Agent's responsibilities

The Agent shall represent no other local or foreign company manufacturing or selling brickmaking machines. The Agent shall set up an appropriate commercial and financial organization and use its best endeavors to promote the sale of the products throughout the territory in a maximum effort to prevent copying of the products.

The Agent shall not disclose any technical or commercial information regarding the products that would weaken the product's position in their life cycle. Moreover, the Agent shall help the customer in the best way to be provided with all the necessary papers such as e.g.

import licenses, feasibility studies, etc. as well as to find adequate financing for the project.

Article 5: Information to the manufacturer

The Agent shall keep the Company currently informed about the market trend, the laws and regulations in force in the Territory to which the products must be conform (e.g. concerning labeling, composition, technical specifications, import duties and regulations, etc.)

Article 6: Information to the Agent

The Company shall keep the Agent currently informed about any modification relative to price, delivery time and terms of payment.

Article 7: Exclusivity

The Company shall not appoint any other agent for the sale of the products in the territory for an indefinite period provided the following requirements are complied with:

11/8/90 (12 months): reception by our bank of irrevocable letters of credit for 10 automatic presses CERAMATIC.

From 11/8/90 on: yearly minimum turnover (to be calculated from the 11/8/90 ofeach year) of 15 CERAMATIC or at least the corresponding value of those products in Belgian Francs.

If the Agent does not attain the fixed objectives, at the end of any of these dead lines, the Company shall be entitled, subject to giving a three month notice to cancel the Agent's exclusivity. The notice will be sent by registered mail.

Article 8: Arbitration

The Geneva (Switzerland) competent law courts shall have jurisdiction in any action arising out or in connection with the present agreement, such jurisdiction shall be exclusive.

Article 9: Sale material

The Company shall provide the Agent free of charge with such quantities of the Company's trade publications and such technical information and advice as shall in the Company's opinion be reasonable, provided always that all such trade publications and trade samples shall remain the property of the Company until and unless given to customers or potential customers.

Article 10: Duration and termination

The present Agreement is stipulated to for an indefinite period and enters into force on the 11/8/90.

This Agreement can be terminated according to the conditions stipulated under art.7 about the company's conditions to the Agent's exclusively.

Either party can also terminate the contract by written notice sent six months before the termination date. The notice will be sent by registered mail.

Article 11: Prohibition of Assignment

The rights conferred on the Agent by this Agreement are not assignable or transferable without the written consent of the Company.

Article 12: Addition and modification

No addition or amendment to the present contract shall be valid unless made in writing and approved by both parties.

Made in duplicate, each party receiving one copy.

The Agent   The Company

Authorized Signing Officer   Authorized Signing Officer

Chapter VI

HOW TO CHECK INCOMING LETTERS OF CREDIT & PREPARE DOCUMENTS FOR THE BANK

Paying attention to detail brings into focus the big picture. In letters of credit a coma or a period may be the difference between collecting a million or losing a million.

—Djora Djabladze

This resource section provides a practical guide to completing a transaction using documentary credits. A general checklist for the seller is followed by a number of sample documents which are frequently required in international trade. The corresponding document checklists should enable you to prepare the necessary documents to meet the conditions of a letter of credit. It may be, however, that the documentary credits in question will exclude certain stipulations or prescribe additional requirements. Please take these individual requirements into account when preparing your documents.

CHECKLIST FOR THE SELLER AFTER RECEIVING A DOCUMENTARY CREDIT

General Points

- Does the documentary credit correspond with the contract, especially in connection with the following points?
  - Amount/unit price
  - Period of validity/time limit for shipping
  - Terms of delivery
  - Description and origin of the merchandise
- Is the documentary credit revocable, irrevocable/unconfirmed or confirmed?
- Is it transferable, if necessary?
- Where and when is the credit available and payable?
- If unconfirmed or confirmed by a bank abroad, how do you assess the
  - credit risk,
  - conditions in the buying country (political and transfer risks),
  - mailing risk (if credit is available abroad)?
- Are the names and addresses of the applicant and the beneficiary correct?
- Is the documentary credit subject to the ICC's currently valid Uniform Customs and Practice for Documentary Credits?
- Is there sufficient time available to complete attestation and authentication procedures?
- Are declarations requested in the documents which cannot be made?
- Are documents stipulated which are contradictory to the terms of delivery?

- Does the credit stipulate documents which need to be drawn up or countersigned by the buyer or his bank? In such a case, the utilization of the credit depends to a large extent on the goodwill of the buyer.
- Can the required number of specified documents be furnished?

Deadlines and Shipment of Goods
- Can the shipment deadline be met?
- Are the terms regarding the place where the goods are to be taken into possession and the points of departure and arrival feasible?
- Are partshipments and transhipments prohibited contrary to the terms of contract?
- Can the prescribed marks and modes of transport be provided?
- Can the documents be presented in the desired form by the dates specified in the credit? (If the credit stipulates a transport document, the documents have to be presented at the bank not later than 21 days after the issue date of the transport document unless the credit stipulates another time limit).
- Are you familiar with the expressions of time utilized in the credit?

Draft
- Are you absolutely certain about the way the draft should be made out?

Invoice
- Can the description of goods in the invoice be taken word for word from the documentary credit?

Transport documents in general
- If the transport document is not described precisely, banks do not accept any document that

   a) is subject to a charter party (only in the case of seaborne transport),

b) designates loading on deck (only in the case of seaborne transport),

c) stipulates carriage by sailing ship.

d) is issued by a forwarding agent (regardless of mode of transport), except in the case where the forwarding agent is also carrier or agent of an expressly named carrier.

- If goods are exported through the intermediary of a company domiciled abroad (a subsidiary), in some countries the value of the merchandise has to be stated in the transport documents. Does this value correspond to the amount and the currency in your invoice?
- Rail freight: Can the duplicate of the railway bill be obtained?

Marine bill of lading
- The restrictions a), b) and c) listed under "Transport documents in general" are also valid for the marine bill of lading.
- The marine bill of lading should not be issued by a forwarding agent, unless the latter is also a carrier or acts as agent for an expressly named carrier.
- If the bill of lading is to be issued to order of the buyer or is to be made out in his name, it will be extremely difficult to arrange any return of the goods. This point should be taken into full account.
- Do the prescribed freight notations conform to the terms of delivery?

Air waybill
- Air waybills issued by forwarding agents are not accepted by banks unless the forwarders act as carrier or as agents for an expressly named carrier.

Insurance documents

- Can the terms of insurance be fulfilled?
- Are the risks to be covered accurately described in the credit? (Avoid imprecise formulations such as "customary risks" etc.)
- Is the insurance coverage also sufficient to meet your requirements?
- Clarify whether a policy or a certificate is required. (Broker's cover notes will not be accepted by the bank unless expressly permitted in the credit.)

Certificate of Origin

- Are the Chamber of Commerce and a consulate willing to attest or authenticate the statements required to appear on the certificate of origin?
- If legalization is necessary, does the respective country maintain a consulate where needed?
- Can a certificate of origin issued in the country of origin be furnished in time?
- Can the legalization be effected in time?

PREPARING DOCUMENTS FOR THE BANK
UNDER A DOCUMENTARY CREDIT

In what follows, you will find a checklist on the left hand page, which corresponds to the document shown on the right hand page.

Document 6.1: Marine/Ocean Bill of Lading UCPDC Art. 23

Questions:

(1) Does the name of the ship appear?

(2) Are the ports of loading and discharge stated and consistent with the requirements of the documentary credit?

(3) Does the bill of lading bear a date of issue?

(4) Is the issuer

a) the carrier (identifiable as the carrier), or

b) a named agent of the named carrier, or

c) the master (identifiable as the master), or

d) a named agent of the named master?

(if c) or d) applies, the document must indicate the name of the carrier)

(5) Is the bill of lading signed by the issuer?

(6) Does the bill of lading bear an "on board" notation

e) in the pre-printed wording on the bill of lading? (the date of issue of the bill of lading is then deemed to be the date of loading on board)

f) in the form of an added "on board" notation on the bill of lading? (the notation must also indicate the date of loading on board but does not need to be signed)

(7) Does the document indicate the number of original bills of lading issued?

Is the complete set of originals present?

Is the bill of lading "clean," i.e. it does not bear a clause or notation declaring a defective condition in the goods and/or packaging?

(8) Is the bill of lading issued to the correct order party as required by the documentary credit, i.e.

a) to a specific order?

b) to your order? (remember to endorse it)

Are all the other conditions required in the documentary credit such as

(9) Name/Address of the shipper

(10) Name/Address of the consignee (see glossary of terms "Straight bill of lading")

(11) Name/Address of the notify party

(12) Shipping marks

(13) Number of packages

(14) Description of goods

(15) Weight

(16) Freight notations

(17) Additional notations met?

Please also note:

Article 31 (UCPDC 500) "On Deck", "Shipper's Load and Count", "Name of Consignor"

Article 32 (UCPDC 500) Clean Transport Documents

Article 33 (UCPDC 500) Freight Payable/Prepaid Transport Documents

Document 6.1: Marine/Ocean Bill of Lading-UCPDC Art. 23

	Reference No.	31101057
PVC WINDOWS LTD. ⑨ CHAUSSEE DU RISQUONS-TOUT, 219/2 7700 MOUSCRON, BELGIUM	ΞΕЅΞΟ	ESTONIAN SHIPPING COMPANY FINBEST LINE SWEBEST LINE

Consignee
GRAND-SERVICE
⑧ DOBROLUBOVA PROEZD D.3 ⑩
MOSCOW 127254
RUSSIA

Notify address
⑪ SAME AS ABOVE

Pre-carriage by* CANMAR FORTUNE V.28	Place of receipt by pre-carrier* MONTREAL
Vessel KXUNGA/SUB ①	Port of loading MONTREAL ②
Port of discharge HELSINKI ②	Place of delivery by on-carrier* DOOR MOSCOW (VIA TRUCK)

Marks and Nos.	Number and kind of packages; description of goods	Gross weight	Measurement
⑫ SCZU 323204-3 SEAL 1909857	1 X40'CNTR STC: ⑭ PARTS FOR ASSEMBLY OF WINDOWS ABOUT 2000 M2; 365 BOXES ⑬ HS: 940600900 [LICENSE #225/900274- ATTACHED] DELIVER CARGO TO TERMINAL GRAND SERVICE DOBROLUBOVA PROEZD D.3 MOSCOW 127254 RUSSIA ⑰	30902 ⑮	LB

ONCARRIAGE BY: VICTOR EK 00161 HELSINKI/HELSINGFORS PL/PB 169
KANAVARANTA/KANALKAJEN 9; TEL: 90.12511; FAX: 90.179.294 ATTN: HANNU KIVISALO

LOADED ON BOARD ⑥
SHIPPERS LOAD STOW AND COUNT *J.S.* OCTOBER 20, 1996 ORIGINAL

Particulars furnished by the Merchant

Freight details, charges etc.
CONTAINER DEMURRAGE, DETENTION, STORAGE CHARGES
TO BE PAID BY PARTY RESPONSIBLE PER CONTAINER PER DAY;
FIRST 7 RUNNING DAYS - FREE, NATIONAL HOLIDAYS EXCLUDED;
NEXT 7 RUNNING DAYS: LINER CNTR DEMURRAGE US $6.00/20'; US $10.00/40';
          THEREAFTER: US $10.00/20'; US $20.00/40';
          SEA PORT STORAGE: US $4.00/20'; US $8.00/40';
DOOR DELIVERY CONTAINERS: TO BE DESTUFFED WITHIN 24 HOURS;
THEREAFTER: US $200.00/CNTR/DAY

FREIGHT PREPAID ⑯
THC   HELSINKI   PREPAID

SHIPPED on board in apparent good order and condition, weight, measure, marks, numbers, quality, contents and value unknown, for carriage to the Port of Discharge or so near thereunto as the Vessel may safely get and lie always afloat, to be delivered in the like good order and condition at the aforesaid Port to Consignees or their Assigns, they paying freight as indicated to the left plus other charges incurred in accordance with the provisions contained in this Bill of Lading. In accepting this Bill of Lading the Merchant expressly accepts and agrees to all its stipulations on both pages, whether written, printed, stamped or otherwise incorporated, as fully as if they were all signed by the Merchant.
One original Bill of Lading must be surrendered duly endorsed in exchange for the goods or delivery order.
I N W I T N E S S whereof the Master of the said Vessel has signed the number of original Bills of Lading stated below, all of this tenor and date, one of which being accomplished, the others to stand void.

* Applicable only when document used as a Through Bill of Lading	Freight payable at TORONTO	Place and date of issue TORONTO OCTOBER 20, 1996 ③
	Number of original Bs/L 3 ⑦	Signature ④ Admiral Navigation Ltd AS AGENTS ONLY ⑤

Document 6.2: Non-Negotiable Sea Waybill
UCPDC Art. 24

In contrast to the marine/ocean bill of lading the non-negotiable sea waybill is not a title document.

Questions:

(1) Does the name of the ship appear?

(2) Are the ports of loading and discharge stated and consistent with the documentary credit regulations?

(3) Does the non-negotiable sea waybill bear a date of issue?

(4) Is the issuer

    a) the carrier (identifiable as the carrier), or

    b) a named agent of the named carrier, or

    c) the captain (identifiable as the captain), or

    d) a named agent of the named captain?

    (if c) or d) applies, the document must indicate the name of the carrier)

(5) Is the non-negotiable sea waybill signed by the issuer?

(6) Does the non-negotiable sea waybill bear an "on board" notation

    a) in the pre-printed wording of the non-negotiable sea waybill?
    (the date of issue of the non-negotiable sea waybill is considered the date of loading on board)

    b) in the form of an added "on board" notation on the non-negotiable sea waybill
    (the notation must also indicate the date of loading on board but does not need to be signed)

    Is the non-negotiable sea waybill "clean", i.e. it does not bear a clause or notation regarding a defective condition in the goods and/or packaging?

    Are all the other conditions required in the documentary credit such as

(7) Name/Address of the shipper

(8) Name/Address of the consignee

(9) Name/Address of the notify party

(10) Shipping marks

(11) Number of packages

(12) Description of goods

(13) Weight

(14) Freight notations

(15) Additional notations met?

Please also note:

Article 31 (UCPDC 500) "On Deck" , "Shipper's Load and Count" , "Name of Consignor"

Article 32 (UCPDC 500) Clean Transport Documents

Article 33 (UCPDC 500) Freight Payable/Prepaid Transport Documents

Document 6.2: Non-Negotiable Sea Waybill - UCPDC Art. 24

Shipper	LINER BILL OF LADING	B/L No.
PVC WINDOWS LTD. **7** CHAUSSEE DU RISQUONS-TOUT, 219/2 7700 MOUSCRON, BELGIUM	Reference No. ≡E**ʃ**O ESTONIAN SHIPPING COMPANY FINBEST LINE SWEBEST LINE	31101057

Consignee
GRAND-SERVICE **8** DOBROLUBOVA PROEZD D.3 MOSCOW 127254 RUSSIA

Notify address
SAME AS ABOVE **9**

Pre-carriage by*	Place of receipt by pre-carrier*
CANMAR FORTUNE V.28	MONTREAL
Vessel K.KUNGA/SUB **1**	Port of receipt MONTREAL **2**
Port of discharge HELSINKI	Place of delivery by on-carrier* DOOR MOSCOW (VIA TRUCK)

Marks and Nos.	Number and kind of packages; description of goods	Gross weight	Measurement
SCZU 323204-3 SEAL 1909857 **10**	1 X40'CNTR STC: **12** PARTS FOR ASSEMBLY OF WINDOWS ABOUT 2000 M2; 365 BOXES **11** HS: 940600900 [LICENSE #225/900274- ATTACHED] DELIVER CARGO TO TERMINAL GRAND SERVICE DOBROLUBOVA PROEZD D.3 MOSCOW 127254 RUSSIA **15**	30902 **13**	LB

ONCARRIAGE BY: VICTOR EK 00161 HELSINKI/HELSINGFORS PL/PB 169
KANAVARANTA/KANALKAJEN 9; TEL: 90.12511; FAX: 90.179.294 ATTN: HANNU KIVISALO

LOADED ON BOARD **6**
SHIPPERS LOAD STOW AND COUNT   OCTOBER 20, 1996

COPY NOT NEGOTIABLE

Particulars furnished by the Merchant

Freight details, charges etc.	
CONTAINER DEMURRAGE, DETENTION, STORAGE CHARGES TO BE PAID BY PARTY RESPONSIBLE PER CONTAINER PER DAY: FIRST 7 RUNNING DAYS - FREE, NATIONAL HOLIDAYS EXCLUDED; NEXT 7 RUNNING DAYS: LINER CNTR DEMURRAGE US $5.00/20'; US $10.00/40' THEREAFTER: US $10.00/20'; US $20.00/40'; SEA PORT STORAGE: US $4.00/20'; US $8.00/40'; DOOR DELIVERY CONTAINERS: TO BE DESTUFFED WITHIN 24 HOURS; THEREAFTER: US $200.00/CNTR/DAY	**SHIPPED** on board in apparent good order and con- dition, weight, measure, marks, numbers, quality, contents and value unknown, for carriage to the Port of Discharge or so near thereunto as the Vessel may safely get and lie always afloat. to be delivered in the like good order and condition at the aforesaid Port unto Consignees or their Assigns, they paying freight as indicated to the left plus other charges incurred in accordance with the provisions contained in this Bill of Lading. In accepting this Bill of Lading the Merchant expressly ac- cepts and agrees to all its stipulations on both pages, whether written, printed, stamped or otherwise incorporated, as fully as if they were all signed by the Merchant. One original Bill of Lading must be surrendered duly endorsed in exchange for the goods or delivery order. IN WITNESS whereof the Master of the said Vessel has signed the number of original Bills of Lading stated below. all of this tenor and date, one of which being accomplished. the others to stand void.
FREIGHT PREPAID **14**	
THC HELSINKI PREPAID Daily demurrage rate (additional Clause A)	

* Applicable only when document used as a Through Bill of Lading	Freight payable at TORONTO	Place and date of issue TORONTO OCTOBER 20, 1996 **3**
	Number of original Bs/L 3	Signature **Admiral Navigation Ltd.** **4** **5** AS AGENTS ONLY

Document 6.3: Charter Party Bill of Lading UCPDC Art. 25

Questions:

(1) Does the name of the ship appear?

(2) Are the ports of loading and discharge stated and consistent with the documentary credit regulations?

(3) Does the bill of lading bear a date of issue? Is the issuer

a) the master (identifiable as the master), or

b) a named agent of the named master, or

c) the owner of the ship (identifiable as the owner), or

d) a named agent of the named captain?

(5) Is the bill of lading signed by the issuer?

(6) Does the bill of lading indicate that it is subject to a charter party?

(7) Does the bill of lading bear an "on board" notation?

a) in the pre-printed wording of the bill of lading? (the date of issue of the bill of lading is deemed to be the date of loading on board)

b) in the form of an added "on board" notation of the bill of lading? (the notation must also indicate the date of loading on board but does not need to be signed)

(8) Does the document indicate the number of originals in which it was issued?

Is the complete set of originals present

Is the bill of lading "clean", i.e. it does not bear a clause or notation regarding defective condition in the goods and/or packaging?

(9) Is the bill of lading issued to the order as required in the documentary credit, i.e.

a) to a specific order?

b) to your order? (remember to endorse it)

Are all the other conditions required in the documentary credit such as

(10) Name/Address of the shipper

(11) Name/Address of the consignee

(12) Name/Address of the notify party

(13) Shipping marks

(14) Number of packages

(15) Description of goods

(16) Weight

(17) Freight notations

(18) Additional notations met?

Please also note:

Article 31 (UCPDC 500) "On Deck" , "Shipper's Load and Count" , "Name of Consignor"

Article 32 (UCPDC 500) Clean Transport Documents

Article 33 (UCPDC 500) Freight Payable/Prepaid Transport Documents

General remarks:

From a documentary credit point of view there is no difference between the Charter Party Bill of Lading and the Marine/Ocean Bill of Lading. In accordance with ICC guidelines, however, the document has to contain an indication that it is subject to a charter party. Please note that UCPDC Art. 25 does not refer to transhipment.

Document 6.3: Charter Party Bill of Lading - UCPDC Art. 25

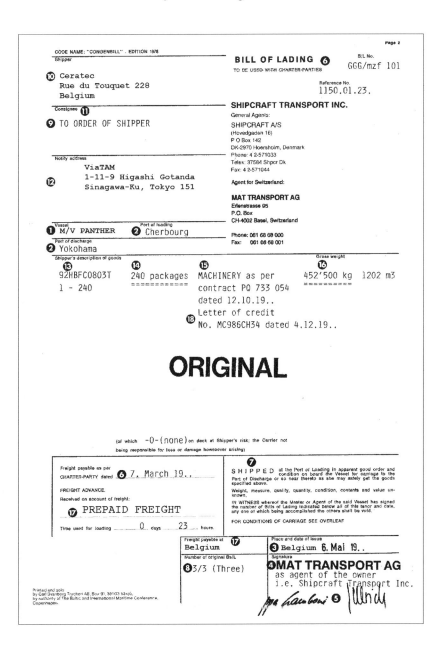

Document 6.4: Multimodal Transport Document UCPDC Art. 26

Questions:

(1) Are the place of dispatch, taking in charge or port of loading, and place of delivery stated and consistent with the documentary credit conditions?

(2) Does the document indicate the name of the carrier or multimodal transport operator?

(3) Has the document been signed by

a) the carrier or multimodal transport operator (identifiable as the carrier or multimodal transport operator), or

b) a named agent of the named carrier or multimodal transport operator, or

c) the master (identifiable as the master), or

d) a named agent of the named master?

(4) Does the document evidence that the goods have been dispatched, taken in charge, or loaded on board?

Does the document bear a date of issue? (deemed to be the date of dispatch, taking in charge or loading on board, and date of shipment unless separately indicated in the document)

Does the document indicate the number of originals in which it was issued, if more than one original was issued?

If applicable, is the complete set of originals present?

(5) If issued in negotiable form, does the document indicate the order party required in the documentary credit, i.e.

a) to a specific order?

b) to your order? (remember to endorse it)

Are all the other conditions required in the documentary credit such as

(6) Name/Address of the shipper

(7) Name/Address of the consignee

(8) Name/Address of the notify party

(9) Shipping marks

(10) Number of packages

(11) Description of goods

(12) Weight

(13) Freight notations met?

Please also note:

Article 27 (UCPDC 500) Air Transport Document

Article 28 (UCPDC 500) Road, Rail or Inland Waterway Transport Documents

Article 30 (UCPDC 500) Transport Documents issued by Freight Forwarders

Article 31 (UCPDC 500) "On Deck", "Shipper's Load and Count", "Name of Consignor"

Article 32 (UCPDC 500) Clean Transport Documents

Article 33 (UCPDC 500) Freight Payable/Prepaid Transport Documents

General remarks:

The document must indicate at least two different modes of transport.

The document may contain the term "intended" in relation to the ship, port of loading, or port of discharge as long as this is not prohibited by the documentary credit.

166

Document 6.4: Multimodal Transport Document - UCPDC Art. 26

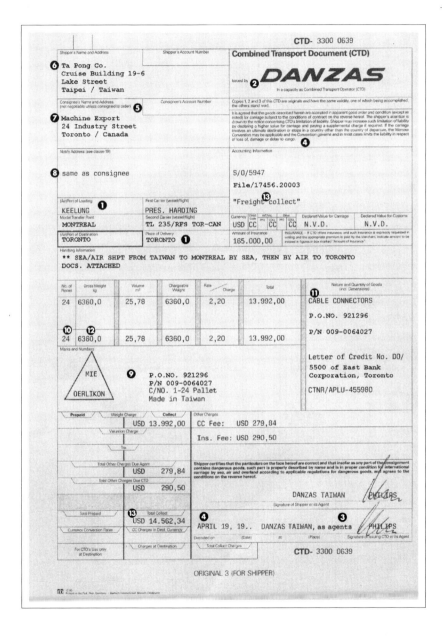

Document 6.5: Air Transport Document
UCPDC Art. 27

Questions:

(1) Are the airports of departure and destination stated and consistent with the documentary credit conditions?

(2) Is the issuer

a) the carrier (identifiable as the carrier), or

b) a named agent of the named carrier?

(3) Is the document signed by the issuer?

(4) Does the document bear a date of issue? (deemed to be the flight date unless otherwise indicated with a specific notation).

(5) Does the document indicate that the goods have been accepted for carriage?

(6) Is the document presented the original for the consignee/shipper?

Are all the other conditions required in the documentary credit such as

(7) Name/Address of the shipper

(8) Name/Address of the consignee

(9) Name/Address of the notify party

(10) Shipping marks

(11) Number of packages

(12) Description of goods

(13) Weight

(14) Freight notations met?

Please also note:

Article 32 (UCPDC 500) Clean Transport Documents

Article 33 (UCPDC 500) Freight Payable/Prepaid Transport Documents

Article 27 a iii. (UCPDC 500) referring to Airway Bills calling for an actual date of dispatch or flight date.

Document 6.5: Air Transport Document - UCPDC Art. 27

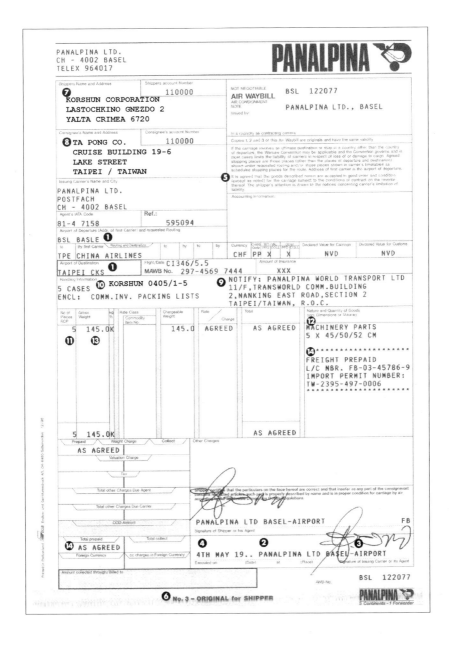

Document 6.6: Courier and Post Receipts
UCPDC Art. 29

Questions:

(1) Is the name of the issuer stated?

(2) Does the document bear the stamped or otherwise authenticated signature of the issuer?

(3) Does the document bear a date of receipt or dispatch? (deemed to be the date of shipment or dispatch)

Are all the other conditions required in the documentary credit such as

(4) Name/Address of the consignee

(5) Freight notations

(6) Place of shipment etc. met?

Document 6.6: Courier and Post Receipts - UCPDC Art. 29

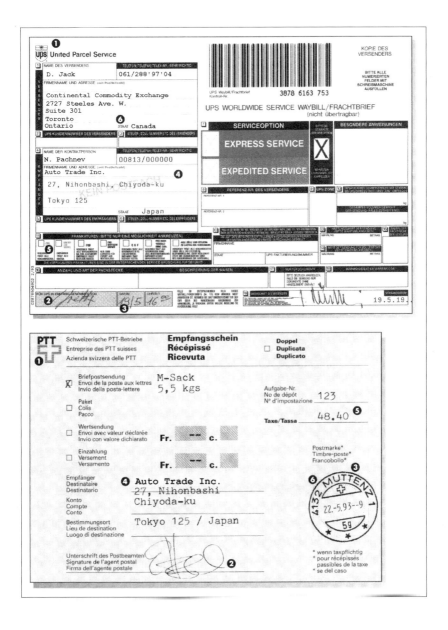

Document 6.7: Transport Documents Issued by Freight Forwarders - UCPDC Art. 30

Questions:

(1)   Is the named issuer (freight forwarder) acting

      a) as the carrier or the multimodal transport operator, or

      b) as a named agent of the named carrier or multimodal transport operator?

(2)   Is the document signed by the issuer?

(3)   Does the document bear a date of issue? (deemed to be the shipment date)

Are all the other conditions required in the documentary credit such as

(4)   Name/Address of the shipper

(5)   Name/Address of the consignee or order party (specific or your order)

(6)   Name/Address of the notify party

(7)   Places of shipment and discharge

(8)   Shipping marks

(9)   Number of packages

(10) Description of goods

(11) Weight

(12) Freight notations met?

Please also note:

      Article 32 (UCPDC 500) Clean Transport Documents

      Article 33 (UCPDC 500) Freight Payable/Prepaid Transport Documents

Document 6.7: Transport Documents Issued by Freight Forwarders - UCPDC Art. 30

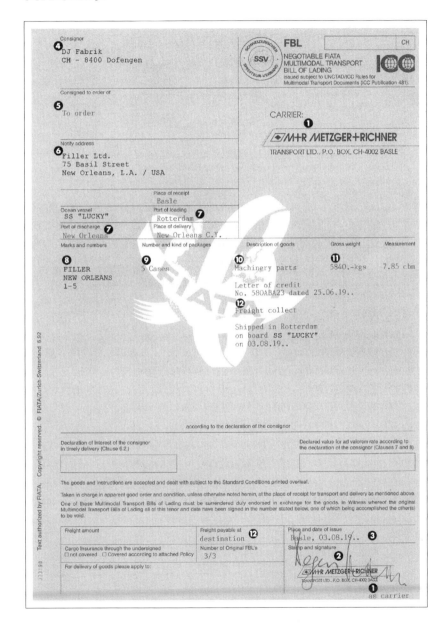

Document 6.8: Insurance Document
UCPDC Art. 34, 35, 36

Questions:

(1)   Was the insurance document issued as a policy or certificate in compliance with the documentary credit stipulations?

(2)   Have all issued originals of the insurance document been presented?

(3)   Is the insurance document issued and signed by an insurance company or underwriter or their agents? Confirmation of cover from insurance brokers will be rejected by the banks.

(4)   Is the insurance document correctly dated and signed?

   Note: The insurance document may not be issued at a date later than the date of loading on board, etc., as indicated on the corresponding shipping document, unless the insurance document specifically states that cover takes effect on the day of shipment at the latest.

(5)   Is the information regarding the transport route and mode of transport consistent with the documentary credit?

(6)   Is the amount insured sufficient and the value correct? (at least 110% of the CIF or CIP value unless a higher insurance is required by the documentary credit).

   See UCPDC Art. 34 f.ii., if the CIF/CIP value cannot be determined.

(7)   The insurance currency must be consistent with that of the documentary credit unless otherwise stated.

(8)   Does the insurance cover all risks as required in the documentary credit? If the documentary credit states "Insurance against all risks", an insurance document with the notation "all risks" is accepted, even if it is stated that certain risks are excluded.

Is the insurance certificate correctly endorsed, if endorsement is required?

Please also note:

   Article 35 (UCPDC 500) Type of Insurance Cover

   Article 36 (UCPDC 500) All Risks Insurance Cover

   Endorsement see glossary

Document 6.8: Insurance Document - UCPDC Art. 34, 35, 36

BLACK SEA AND BALTIC
GENERAL INSURANCE COMPANY LIMITED

65 FENCHURCH STREET, LONDON EC3M 4EY

❶ *Certificate* N⁰ 78607

❼
£X.CAD.100,000....

It is hereby certified that this Company has insured under *Open Cover/Policy No...*96G590X0038
in the sum of ..ONE HUNDRED THOUSAND CANADIAN DOLLARS ❻ ....
in favour of ...HARTE.&.LYNE..
who have deposited a/*the said* policy covering this certificate with this Company on behalf of all
parties interested and have requested this Company to pay any claim arising under the said policy in
respect of the said interest to their order.

In accordance with the above request this Company will pay, on production of the Invoices
and Bills of Lading, and in exchange for this Certificate, both fully endorsed, any lawful claim
arising on said Policy in respect of the interest insured thereunder, it being understood that notice
of such claim be given by the holder of this Certificate to this Company as soon as practicable.

It is agreed by the holder of this Certificate that in the event of loss or damage notice in writing
shall be given to the Company.

Vessel   CM FORTUNE &/OR
          STEAMERS &/OR CONVEYANCES
❺ Voyage
          MONTREAL, QUEBEC, CANADA TO ROUZA HOUSE, TUCHKOVO, MOSCOW REGION
Interest insured

          40' CONTAINER SAID TO CONTAIN WINDOW ASSEMBLIES (NO GLASS)
          CONTAINER NO: SCZU 323204 (3)
          SEAL NO: 1909857

Conditions

          AS ATTACHED

Countersigned this 19TH day   *For and on behalf of*
❹ of OCTOBER   1996 **BLACK SEA AND BALTIC GENERAL INSURANCE COMPANY LIMITED**
❷ ISSUED IN 2 ORIGINALS

                                                   ❸
                                      D. J. SMITH
                                      Underwriter
T.C.P. LTD.

Attaching to and forming part of Certificate Number 78607 in the name of Harte & Lynne.

❽ CONDITIONS
Against All risks of physical loss &/or damage, subject to the Conditions and Exclusions of the
Institute Cargo Clauses (A) 1.1.82. CL 252 &/or Institute Cargo Clauses (Air) CL 259 1.1.82.
Including Institute Strikes Clauses (Cargo) 1.1.82. CL 255 Including Institute War Clauses (Cargo)
1.1.82. CL 255, 257, or 258 as applicable. Institute Classification Clause CL 354 13.4.92. Institute
Radioactive Contamination Exclusion Clause (CL 356) 1.10.90. General average and salvage
charges payable as provided in the contract of affreightment. For the purpose of claims for general
average contribution and salvage charges recoverable hereunder the subject-matter insured shall
be deemed to be insured for its full contributory value. General average deposits payable on
production of general average deposit receipts. Warranted no known or reported losses as at 24th
October 1996. Deductible CAD 500 each & every loss.

Document 6.9: Commercial Invoice - UCPDC Art. 37

Questions:

(1) Is the invoice issued by the beneficiary as stated in the documentary credit?

(2) Is the invoice issued to the purchaser (applicant) named in the documentary credit?

Does the address in the invoice match that in the documentary credit?

(3) Does the description of the goods correspond exactly to that stated in the documentary credit?

(4) Does the value of the goods and/or unit price match that of the documentary credit as regards the amount/currency?

(5) Are the delivery conditions (CIF/FOB, etc.) listed in the invoice?

Are these consistent with the documentary credit conditions?

(6) Is the invoice signed, if required by the documentary credit?

Are any certification/legalizations required in the documentary credit present?

Are special conditions required in the documentary credit (customs tariff number, licence number, etc.) indicated on the invoice?

Document 6.9: Commercial Invoice - UCPDC Art. 37

Invoice

Date: October 20, 1996

From: ❶	**To:** ❷
B&B Trading International Corp. 2727 Steeles Ave. W., Suite 301 Ontario, Canada M3J 3G9	Grand-Service Dobrolubova Proezd D.3 Moscow 127254 Russia

COMMERCIAL INVOICE NO. 9609.4

Description	Number of Boxes
PARTS FOR ASSEMBLY OF WINDOWS ABOUT 2000M² ❸	365 boxes
	❹
❺ **CIP Moscow TOTAL**	Cdn $45,000.00

❻ _____
Authorized Signing Officer
B&B Trading International Corp.

Document 6.10: Other Documents

If documentary credits require other documents in addition to the invoice, transport and insurance documents, the text of the documentary credit should state the issuer and contents of such additional documents.

If the documentary credit does not indicate the issuer of such documents and their content, the banks will accept these documents as presented, provided that their data content is not inconsistent with any other stipulated documents and that they do not contradict the other conditions of the documentary credit and the UCPDC.

See UCPDC Art. 20, 21, 22 and 38.

Please ensure that the other documents are consistent with the documentary credit conditions in the following points:

(1) Name/Address of the shipper

Name/Address of the consignee

Description of the goods

Country of origin/destination

Additional notations (e.g. number of documentary credit)

Issuer

Certification/Legalizations

Shipping marks

Weight, volume, number of packages

General remarks:

Certificates must usually bear the signature of the issuer.

Documents must be consistent with one another.

The number of packages, gross and net weight, etc. must be the same on all documents.

Document 6.10: Other Documents

CERTIFICATE OF ORIGIN

SHIPPER/EXPORTER (COMPLETE NAME AND ADDRESS)	Reference Nos.		
B&B TRADING INTERNATIONAL CORP. 2727 STEELES AVENUE WEST 3RD FLOOR ❶ TORONTO, ONTARIO, CANADA	OCEAN BOOKING	BILL OF LADING NO	
	TO4615AN	056TOOK084	
	NAME OF AUTHORIZED TRADE ASSOSIATION		
CONSIGNEE(COMPLETE NAME AND ADDRESS)			
PLANETA SHELKOVO CITY, MOSCOW REGION ZARECHNAYA STR. 127 ❷ RUSSIA			
PRECARRIAGE BY			
CANMAR			
VESSEL C.M.ENDEAVOUR	VOY. 34		

MARKS & NUMBERS	DESCRIPTION OF PACKAGES AND GOODS	QUANTITY	GROSS WEIGHT(KGR)
1 /40' ❽ CAXU 4215320 SEAL# 240122	S.T.C. 564 BOXES AND BUNDLES PLASTIC PARTS FOR ASSEMBLY OF PVC WINDOWS AND TOOLING ❸	1 ❾	18322

❺ DOCUMENTARY CREDIT NO. 2361

WE HEREBY CERTIFIED THAT THE ABOVE MENTIONED GOODS ORIGINATED IN :

CANADA ❹

SWORN TO ME THIS 25 DAY OF AUGUST 1997

SIGNATURE ❻

PLACE AND DATE: TORONTO 25 AUGUST 1997

THE UNDERSIGNED HAS EXAMINED THE MANUFACTURES INVOICE OR SHIPPER'S AFFIDAVIT CONCERNING THE ORIGIN OF THE MERCHANDISE, AND ACCORDING TO THE BEST OF HIS KNOWLEDGE AND BELIEF FINDS THAT THE PRODUCTS ORIGINATED IN :

CANADA ❼

AUTHORIZED SIGNATURE

AUTHORIZED SIGNATURE

Chapter VII

UNIFORM CUSTOMS AND PRACTICE FOR DOCUMENTARY CREDITS PUBLICATION [UCPDC 500]

Uniform Customs and Practice for Documentary Credits Publication [UCPDC 500] is the law governing letters of credit. Banks constantly refer to UCPDC 500 when issuing documentary credits and checking documents presented under credits issued in accordance with UCP 500 rules. Please read carefully all articles of UCP and understand them prior to issuing or negotiating a letter of credit.

A. General Provisions and Definitions

Article 1 - Application of UCP

The Uniform Customs and Practice for Documentary Credits, 1993 Revision, ICC Publication No.500, shall apply to all Documentary Credits (including to the extent to which they may be applicable, Standby Letter(s) of Credit) where they are incorporated into the text of the Credit. They are binding on all parties thereto, unless otherwise expressly stipulated in the credit.

Article 2 - Meaning of Credit

For the purposes of these Articles, the expressions "Documentary Credit(s)" and "Standby Letters(s) of Credit" (hereinafter referred to as "Credit(s)"), mean any arrangement, however named or described, whereby a bank (the "Issuing Bank") acting at the request and on the instructions of a customer (the "Applicant") or on its own behalf,

i   is to make a payment to or to the order of a third party (the "Beneficiary"), or is to accept and pay bills of exchange (Draft(s)) drawn by the Beneficiary,

or

ii   authorizes another bank to effect such payment, or to accept and pay such bills of exchange (Draft(s)),

or

iii   authorizes another bank to negotiate, against stipulated document(s), provided that the terms and conditions of the Credit are complied with.

For the purposes of these Articles, branches of a bank in different countries are considered another bank.

Article 3 - Credits v. Contracts

a   Credits, by their nature, are separate transactions from the sales or other contract(s) on which they may be based and banks are in no way concerned with or bound by such contract(s), even if any reference whatsoever to such contract(s) is included in the Credit. Consequently, the undertaking of a bank to pay, accept and pay Draft(s) or negotiate and/or to fulfil any other obligation under the Credit, is not subject to claims or defences by the Applicant resulting from his relations with the Issuing Bank or the Beneficiary.

b   A Beneficiary can in no case avail himself of the contractual relationships existing between the banks or between the Applicant and the Issuing Bank.

Article 4 - Documents v. Goods/Services/Performances

In Credit operations all parties concerned deal with documents, and not with goods, services and/or other performances to which the documents may relate.

Article 5 - Instructions to Issue/Amend Credits

a   Instructions for the issuance of a Credit, the Credit itself, instructions for an amendment thereto, and the amendment itself, must be complete and precise.

In order to guard against confusion and misunderstanding, banks should discourage any attempt:
i   to include excessive detail in the Credit or in any amendment thereto;
ii to give instructions to issue, advise or confirm a Credit by reference to a Credit previously issued (similar Credit) where such previous Credit has been subject to accepted amendment(s), and/or unaccepted amendment(s).

b   All instructions for the issuance of a Credit and the Credit itself and, where applicable, all instructions for an amendment thereto and the amendment itself, must state precisely the document(s) against which payment, acceptance or negotiation is to be made.

B. Form and Notification of Credits

Article 6 – Revocable v. Irrevocable Credits

a   A Credit may be either

   i   revocable,

   or

   ii irrevocable.

b   The Credit, therefore, should clearly indicate whether it is revocable or irrevocable.

c   In the absence of such indication the Credit shall be deemed to be irrevocable.

Article 7 – Advising Bank's Liability

a   A Credit may be advised to a Beneficiary through another bank (the "Advising Bank") without engagement on the part of the Advising Bank, but that Bank, if it elects to advise the Credit, shall take reasonable care to check the apparent authenticity of the Credit which it advises. If the bank elects not to advise the Credit, it must so inform the Issuing Bank without delay.

b   If the Advising Bank cannot establish such apparent authenticity it must inform, without delay, the bank from which the instructions appear to have been received that it has been unable to establish the authenticity of the Credit and if it elects nonetheless to advise the Credit it must inform the Beneficiary that it has not been able to establish the authenticity of the Credit.

Article 8 – Revocation of a Credit

a   A revocable Credit may be amended or canceled by the Issuing Bank at any moment and without prior notice to the Beneficiary.

b   However, the Issuing Bank must:

   i   reimburse another bank with which a revocable Credit has been made available for sight payment, acceptance or negotiation - for any payment, acceptance or negotiation made by such bank - prior to receipt by it of notice of amendment or cancellation, against documents which appear on their face to be in compliance with the terms and conditions of the Credit;

ii reimburse another bank with which a revocable Credit has been made available for deferred payment, if such a bank has, prior to receipt by it of notice of amendment or cancellation, taken up documents which appear on their face to be in compliance with the terms and conditions of the Credit.

Article 9 – Liability of Issuing and Confirming Banks

a An irrevocable Credit constitutes a definite undertaking of the Issuing Bank, provided that the stipulated documents are presented to the Nominated Bank or to the Issuing bank and that the terms and conditions of the Credit are complied with:

i if the Credit provides for sight payment, - to pay at sight;

ii if the Credit provides for deferred payment - to pay on the maturity date(s) determinable in accordance with the stipulations of the Credit;

iii if the Credit provides for acceptance:

a by the Issuing Bank - to accept Draft(s) drawn by the Beneficiary on the Issuing Bank and pay them at maturity, or

b by another drawee bank - to accept and pay at maturity Draft(s) drawn by the Beneficiary on the Issuing Bank in the event the drawee bank stipulated in the Credit does not accept Draft(s) drawn on it, or pay Draft(s) accepted but not paid by such drawee bank at maturity;

iv if the Credit provides for negotiation - to pay without recourse to drawers and/or bona fide holders, Draft(s) drawn by the Beneficiary and/or document(s) presented under the Credit. A Credit should not be issued available by Draft(s) on the Applicant. If the Credit nevertheless calls for Draft(s) on the Applicant, banks will consider such Draft(s) as an additional document(s).

b A confirmation of an irrevocable Credit by another bank (the "Confirming Bank") upon the authorization or request of the

184

Issuing Bank, constitutes a definite undertaking of the Confirming Bank, in addition to that of the issuing Bank, provided that the stipulated documents are presented to the Confirming Bank or to any other Nominated Bank and that the terms and conditions of the Credit are complied with:

i if the Credit provides for sight payment - to pay at sight;

ii if the Credit provides for deferred payment - to pay on the maturity date(s) determinable in accordance with the stipulations of the Credit;

iii if the Credit provides for acceptance:

a by the Confirming Bank - to accept Draft(s) drawn by the Beneficiary on the Confirming Bank and pay them at maturity,

or

b by another drawee bank - to accept and pay at maturity Draft(s) drawn by the Beneficiary on the Confirming Bank, in the event the drawee bank stipulated in the Credit does not accept Draft(s) drawn on it, or to pay Draft(s) accepted but not paid by such drawee bank at maturity;

iv if the Credit provides for negotiation - to negotiate without recourse to drawers and/or bona fide holders, Draft(s) drawn by the Beneficiary and/or document(s) presented under the Credit. A Credit should not be issued available by Draft(s) on the Applicant. If the Credit nevertheless calls for Draft(s) on the Applicant, banks will consider such Draft(s) as an additional document(s).

c i If another bank is authorized or requested by the Issuing Bank to add its confirmation to a Credit but is not prepared to do so, it must so inform the Issuing Bank without delay.

ii Unless the Issuing Bank specifies otherwise in its authorization or request to add confirmation, the Advising Bank may advise the Credit to the Beneficiary without adding its confirmation.

d i Except as otherwise provided by Article 48, an irrevocable Credit can neither be amended nor canceled without the agreement of the Issuing Bank, the Confirming Bank, if any, and the Beneficiary.

ii The Issuing Bank shall be irrevocably bound by an amendment(s) issued by it from the time of the issuance of such amendment(s). A Confirming Bank may extend its confirmation to an amendment and shall be irrevocably bound as of the time of its advice of the amendment. A Confirmation Bank may, however, choose to advise an amendment to the Beneficiary without extending its confirmation and if so, must inform the Issuing Bank and the beneficiary without delay.

iii The terms of the original Credit (or a Credit incorporating previously accepted amendment(s)) will remain in force for the Beneficiary until the beneficiary communicates his acceptance of the amendment to the bank that advised such amendment. The Beneficiary should give notification of acceptance or rejection of amendment(s). If the Beneficiary fails to give such notification, the tender of documents to the Nominated Bank or Issuing Bank, that conform to the Credit and to not yet accepted amendment(s), will be deemed to be notification of acceptance by the Beneficiary of such amendment(s) and as of that moment the Credit will be amended.

iv Partial acceptance of amendments contained in one and the same advice of amendments is not allowed and consequently will not be given any effect.

Article 10 – Types of Credit

a   All Credits must clearly indicate whether they are available by sight payment, by deferred payment, by acceptance or negotiation.

b   i   Unless the Credit stipulates that it is available only with the Issuing Bank, all Credits must nominate the bank (the "Nominated Bank") which is authorized to pay, to incur a deferred payment undertaking, to accept Draft(s) or to negotiate. In a freely negotiable Credit, any bank is a Nominated Bank. Presentation of documents must be made to the Issuing Bank or the Confirming bank, if any, or any other Nominated Bank.

ii   Negotiation means the giving of value for Draft(s) and/or document(s) by the bank authorized to negotiate. Mere examination of the documents without giving of value does not constitute a negotiation.

c   Unless the Nominated Bank is the Confirming Bank, nomination by the Issuing Bank does not constitute any undertaking by the Nominated Bank to pay, to incur a deferred payment undertaking, to accept Draft(s), or to negotiate. Except where expressly agreed to by the Nominated Bank and so communicated to the Beneficiary, the Nominated Bank's receipt of and/or examination and/or forwarding of the documents does not make that bank liable to pay, to incur a deferred payment undertaking, to accept Draft(s), or to negotiate.

d   By nominating another bank, or by allowing for negotiation by any bank, or by authorizing or requesting another bank to add its confirmation, the Issuing Bank authorizes such bank to pay, accept Draft(s) or negotiate as the case may be, against documents which appear on their face to be in compliance with the terms and conditions of the credit and undertakes to reimburse such bank in accordance with the provisions of these Articles.

Article 11 – Teletransmitted and Pre-Advised Credits

a   i   When an Issuing Bank instructs an Advising bank by an authenticated teletransmission to advise a Credit or an amendment to a Credit, the teletransmission will be deemed to be the operative Credit instrument or the operative amendment, and no mail confirmation should be sent. Should a mail confirmation nevertheless be sent, it will have no effect and the Advising Bank will have no obligation to check such mail confirmation against the operative Credit instrument or the operative amendment received by teletransmission.

ii   If the teletransmission states "full details to follow" (or words of similar effect) or states that the mail confirmation is to be the operative Credit instrument or the operative amendment, then the teletransmission will not be deemed to be the operative Credit instrument or the operative amendment. The Issuing Bank must forward the operative Credit instrument or the operative amendment to such Advising Bank without delay.

b   If a bank uses the services of an Advising Bank to have the Credit advised to the Beneficiary, it must also use the services of the same bank for advising an amendment(s).

c   A preliminary advice of the issuance or amendment of an irrevocable Credit (pre-advice), shall only be given by an Issuing Bank if such bank is prepared to issue the operative Credit instrument or the operative amendment thereto. Unless otherwise stated in such preliminary advice by the Issuing Bank, an Issuing Bank having given such pre-advice shall be irrevocably committed to issue or amend the Credit, in terms not inconsistent with the pre-advice, without delay.

Article 12 - Incomplete or Unclear Instructions

If incomplete or unclear instructions are received to advise, confirm or amend a credit, the bank requested to act on such instructions may give preliminary notification to the Beneficiary for information only and without responsibility. This preliminary notification should state clearly that the notification is provided for information only and without the responsibility of the Advising Bank. In any event, the Advising Bank must inform the Issuing bank of the action taken and request it to provide the necessary information.

The Issuing Bank must provide the necessary information without delay. The Credit will be advised, confirmed or amended, only when complete and clear instructions have been received and if the Advising Bank is then prepared to act on the instructions.

C.   Liabilities and Responsibilities

Article 13 - Standard for Examination of Documents

a   Banks must examine all documents stipulated in the Credit with reasonable care to ascertain whether or not they appear, on their face, to be in compliance with the terms and conditions of the Credit. Compliance of the stipulated documents on their face with the terms and conditions of the Credit, shall be determined by international standard banking practice as reflected in these Articles. Documents which appear on their face to be inconsistent with one another will be considered as not appearing on their face to be in compliance with the terms and conditions of the Credit.

Documents not stipulated in the Credit will not be examined by banks. If they receive such documents, they shall return them to the presenter or pass them on without responsibility.

b   The Issuing Bank, the Confirming Bank, if any, or a Nominated Bank acting on their behalf, shall each have a reasonable time, not to exceed seven banking days following the day of receipt of the documents, to examine the documents and determine whether to take up or refuse the documents and to inform the party from which it received the documents accordingly.

c   If a Credit contains conditions without stating the document(s) to be presented in compliance therewith, banks will deem such conditions as not stated and will disregard them.

Article 14 - Discrepant Documents and Notice

a   When the Issuing Bank authorizes another bank to pay, incur a deferred payment undertaking, accept Draft(s), or negotiate against documents which appear on their face to be in compliance with the terms and conditions of the Credit, the Issuing Bank and the Confirming Bank, if any, are bound:
i   to reimburse the Nominated Bank which has paid, incurred a deferred payment undertaking, accepted Draft(s), or negotiated,
ii   to take up the documents.

b   Upon receipt of the documents the Issuing Bank and/or Confirming Bank, if any, or a Nominated Bank acting on their behalf, must determine on the basis of the documents alone whether or not they appear on their face to be in compliance with the terms and conditions of the Credit. If the documents appear on their face not to be in compliance with the terms and conditions of the Credit, such banks may refuse to take up the documents.

c   If the Issuing bank determines that the documents appear on their face not to be in compliance with the terms and conditions of the Credit, it may in its sole judgment approach the Applicant for a waiver of the discrepancy(ies). This does not, however, extend the period mentioned in sub-Article 13 (b).

d   i   If the Issuing Bank and/or Confirming Bank, if any, or a Nominated Bank acting on their behalf, decides to refuse the documents, it must give notice to that effect by telecommunication or, if that is not possible, by other expeditious means, without delay but no later than the close of the seventh banking day following the day of receipt of the documents. Such notice shall be given to the bank from which it received the documents, or to the Beneficiary, if it received the documents directly from him.

ii   Such notice must state all discrepancies in respect of which the bank refuses the documents and must also state whether it is holding the documents at the disposal of, or is returning them to, the presenter.

iii   The Issuing Bank and/or Confirming Bank, if any, shall then be entitled to claim from the remitting bank refund, with interest, or any reimbursement which has been made to that bank.

e   If the Issuing Bank and/or Confirming Bank, if any, fails to act in accordance with the provisions of this Article and/or fails to hold the documents at the disposal of, or return them to the presenter, the Issuing Bank and/or Confirming Bank, if any, shall be precluded from claiming that the documents are not in compliance with the terms and conditions of the Credit.

f   If the remitting bank draws the attention of the Issuing Bank and/or Confirming Bank, if any, to any discrepancy(ies) in the document(s) or advises such banks that it has paid, incurred a deferred payment undertaking, accepted Draft(s) or negotiated under reserve or against an indemnity in respect of such discrepancy(ies), the Issuing Bank and/or Confirming bank, if any, shall not be thereby relieved from any of their obligations under any provision of this Article. Such reserve or indemnity concerns only the relations between the remitting bank and the party towards whom the reserve was made, or from whom, or on whose behalf, the indemnity was obtained.

Article 15 - Disclaimer on Effectiveness of Documents

Banks assume no liability or responsibility for the form, sufficiency, accuracy, genuineness, falsification or legal effect of any document(s), or for the general and/or particular conditions stipulated in the document(s) or superimposed thereon; nor do they assume any liability or responsibility for the description, quantity, weight, quality, condition, packing, delivery, value or existence of the goods represented by any document(s), or for the good faith or acts and/or omissions, solvency, performance or standing of the consignors, the carriers, the forwarders, the consignees or the insurers of the goods, or any other person whomsoever.

Article 16 - Disclaimer on the Transmission of Messages

Banks assume no liability or responsibility for the consequences arising out of delay and/or loss in transit of any message(s), letter(s) or document(s), or for delay, mutilation or other error(s) arising in the transmission of any telecommunication. Banks assume no liability or responsibility for errors in translation and/or interpretation of technical terms, and reserve the right to transmit Credit terms without translating them.

Article 17 - Force Majeure

Banks assume no liability or responsibility for the consequences arising out of the interruption of their business by Acts of God, riots, civil commotions, insurrections, wars or any other causes beyond their control, or by any strikes or lockouts. Unless specifically authorized, banks will not, upon resumption of their business, pay, incur a deferred payment undertaking, accept Draft(s) or negotiate under Credits which expired during such interruption of their business.

Article 18 - <u>Disclaimer for Acts of an Instructed Party</u>

a   Banks utilizing the services of another bank or other banks for the purpose of giving effect to the instructions of the Applicant do so for the account and at the risk of such Applicant.

b   Banks assume no liability or responsibility should the instructions they transmit not be carried out, even if they have themselves taken the initiative in the choice of such other bank(s).

c   i A party instructing another party to perform services is liable for any charges, including commissions, fees, costs or expenses incurred by the instructed party in connection with its instructions.

    ii Where a Credit stipulates that such charges are for the account of a party other than the instructing party, and charges cannot be collected, the instructing party remains ultimately liable for the payment thereof.

d   The Applicant shall be bound by and liable to indemnify the banks against all obligations and responsibilities imposed by foreign laws and usages.

Article 19 - <u>Bank-to-Bank Reimbursement Arrangements</u>

a   If an Issuing Bank intends that the reimbursement to which a paying, accepting or negotiating bank is entitled, shall be obtained by such bank (the "Claiming Bank"), claiming on another party (the "Reimbursing Bank"), it shall provide such Reimbursing Bank in good time with the proper instructions or authorization to honor such reimbursement claims.

b   Issuing Banks shall not require a Claiming Bank to supply a certificate of compliance with the terms and conditions of the Credit to the Reimbursing Bank.

c   An Issuing Bank shall not be relieved from any of its obligations to provide reimbursement if and when reimbursement is not received by the Claiming Bank from the Reimbursement Bank.

d   The Issuing Bank shall be responsible to the Claiming Bank for any loss or interest if reimbursement is not provided by the

Reimbursing Bank on first demand, or as otherwise specified in the Credit, or mutually agreed, as the case may be.

e   The Reimbursing Bank's charges should be for the account of the Issuing Bank. However, in cases where the charges are for the account of another party, it is the responsibility of the Issuing Bank to so indicate in the original Credit and in the reimbursement authorization. In cases where the Reimbursing Bank's charges are for the account of another party they shall be collected from the Claiming Bank when the Credit is drawn under. In cases where the Credit is not drawn under, the Reimbursing Bank's charges remain the obligation of the Issuing Bank.

D. Documents

Article 20 - Ambiguity as to the Issuers of Documents

a   Terms such as "first class", "well known", "qualified", "independent", "official", "competent", "local" and the like, shall not be used to describe the issuers of any document(s) to be presented under a Credit. If such terms are incorporated in the Credit, banks will accept the relative document(s) as presented, provided that it appears on its face to be in compliance with the other terms and conditions of the Credit and not to have been issued by the Beneficiary.

b   Unless otherwise stipulated in the Credit, banks will also accept as an original document(s), a document(s) produced or appearing to have been produced:
i   by reprographic, automated or computerized systems.
ii   as carbon copies, provided that it is marked as original and, where necessary, appears to be signed.
A document may signed by handwriting, by facsimile signature, by perforated signature, by stamp, by symbol, or by any other mechanical or electronic method of authentication.

c   i. Unless otherwise stipulated in the Credit, banks will accept as a copy(ies), a document(s) either labeled copy or not marked as an original - a copy(ies) need not be signed.

ii   Credits that require multiple document(s) such as "duplicate", "two fold", "two copies" and the like, will be satisfied by the presentation of one original and the remaining number in copies except where the document itself indicates otherwise.

d   Unless otherwise stipulated in the Credit, a condition under a credit calling for a document to be authenticated, validated, legalized, visaed, certified or indicating a similar requirement, will be satisfied by any signature, mark, stamp or label on such document that on its face appears to satisfy the above condition.

Article 21 - Unspecified Issuers or Contents of Documents

When documents other than transport documents, insurance documents and commercial invoices are called for, the Credit should stipulate by whom such documents are to be issued and their wording or data content. If the Credit does not so stipulate, banks will accept such documents as presented, provided that their data content is not inconsistent with any other stipulated document presented.

Article 22 - Issuance Date of Documents v. Credit Date

Unless otherwise stipulated in the Credit, banks will accept a document bearing a date of issuance prior to that of the Credit, subject to such document being presented within the time limits set out in the Credit and in these Articles.

Article 23 - Marine/Ocean Bill of Lading

a   If a Credit calls for a bill of lading covering a port-to-port shipment, banks will, unless otherwise stipulated in the Credit, accept a document, however named which:
i   appears on its face to indicate the name of the carrier and to have been signed or otherwise authenticated by:
  • the carrier or a named agent for or on behalf of the carrier, or
  • the master or a named agent for or on behalf of the master.

Any signature or authentication of the carrier or master must be identified as carrier or master, as the case may be. An agent signing or authenticating for the carrier or master must also indicate the name and the capacity of the party, i.e. carrier or master, on whose behalf that agent is acting,

and

ii indicates that the goods have been loaded on board, or shipped on a named vessel.

Loading on board or shipment on a named vessel may be indicated by pre-printed wording on the bill of lading that the goods have been loaded on board a named vessel or shipped on a named vessel, in which case the date of issuance of the bill of lading will be deemed to be the date of loading on board and the date of shipment.

In all other cases loading on board a named vessel must be evidenced by a notation on the bill of lading which gives the date on which the goods have been loaded on board, in which case the date of the on board notation will be deemed to be the date of shipment.

If the bill of lading contains the indication "intended vessel," or similar qualification in relation to the vessel, loading on board a named vessel must be evidenced by an on board notation on the bill of lading which, in addition to the date on which the goods have been loaded on board, also includes the name of the vessel on which the goods have been loaded, even if they have been loaded on the vessel named as the "intended vessel".

If the bill of lading indicates a place of receipt or taking in charge different from the port of loading, the on board notation must also include the port of loading stipulated in the Credit and the name of the vessel on which the goods have been loaded, even if they have been loaded on the vessel named in the bill of lading. This provision also applies whenever loading on board the vessel is indicated by pre-printed wording on the bill of lading,

and

iii indicates the port of loading and the port of discharge stipulated in the Credit, notwithstanding that it:

a indicates a place of taking in charge different from the port of loading, and/or a place of final destination different from the port of discharge,

and/or

b contains the indication "intended" or similar qualification in relation to the port of loading and/or port of discharge, as long as the document also states the ports of loading and/or discharge stipulated in the Credit.

and

iv consists of a sole original bill of lading, or, if issued in more than one original, the full set as so issued,

and

v appears to contain all of the terms and conditions of carriage, or some of such terms and conditions by reference to a source or document other than the bill of lading (short form/ blank back bill of lading); banks will not examine the contents of such terms and conditions,

and

vi contains no indication that it is subject to a charter party and/or no indication that the carrying vessel is propelled by sail only,

and

vii in all other respects meets the stipulations of the Credit.

b For the purpose of this Article, transhipment means unloading and reloading from one vessel to another vessel during the course of ocean carriage from the port of loading to the port of discharge stipulated in the Credit.

c Unless transhipment is prohibited by the terms of the Credit, banks will accept a bill of lading which indicates that the goods will be transhipped, provided that the entire ocean carriage is covered by one and the same bill of lading.

d Even if the Credit prohibits transhipment, banks will accept a bill of lading which:

i indicates that transhipment will take place as long as the relevant cargo is shipped in Container(s), Trailer(s) and/or barge(s) as evidenced by the bill of lading, provided that the

entire ocean carriage is covered by one and the same bill of lading,
and/or
ii incorporates clauses stating that the carrier reserves the right to tranship.

Article 24 - Non-Negotiable Sea Waybill

a   If a Credit calls for a non-negotiable sea waybill covering a port-to-port shipment, banks will, unless otherwise stipulated in the Credit, accept a document, however named, which:
i   appears on its face to indicate the name of the carrier and to have been signed or otherwise authenticated by:
   • the carrier or a named agent for or on behalf of the carrier, or
   • the master or a named agent for or on behalf of the master.
Any signature or authentication of the carrier or master must be identified as carrier or master, as the case may be. An agent signing or authenticating for the carrier or master must also indicate the name and the capacity of the party, i.e. carrier or master, on whose behalf that agent is acting,
and
ii   indicates that the goods have been loaded on board, or shipped on a named vessel.
Loading on board or shipment on a named vessel may be indicated by pre-printed wording on the non-negotiable sea waybill that the goods have been loaded on board a named vessel or shipped on a named vessel, in which case the date of issuance of the non-negotiable sea waybill will be deemed to be the date of loading on board and the date of shipment.
In all other cases loading on board a named vessel must be evidenced by a notation on the non-negotiable sea waybill which gives the date on which the goods have been loaded on board, in which case the date of the on board notation will be deemed to be the date of shipment.
If the non-negotiable sea waybill contains the indication "in-

tended vessel", or similar qualification in relation to the vessel, loading on board a named vessel must be evidenced by an on board notation on the non-negotiable sea waybill which, in addition to the date on which the goods have been loaded on board, includes the name of the vessel on which the goods have been loaded, even if they have been loaded on the vessel named as the "intended vessel".

If the non-negotiable sea waybill indicates a place of receipt or taking in charge different from the port of loading, the on board notation must also include the port of loading stipulated in the Credit and the name of the vessel on which the goods have been loaded, even if they have been loaded on a vessel named in the non-negotiable sea waybill. This provision also applies whenever loading on boarding the vessel is indicated by pre-printed wording on the non-negotiable sea waybill,
and

iii indicates the port of loading and the port of discharge stipulated in the Credit, notwithstanding that it:

a Indicates a place of taking in charge different from the port of loading, and/or a place of final destination different from the port of discharge,
and/or

b contains the indication "intended" or similar qualification in relation to the port of loading and/or port of discharge, as long as the document also states the ports of loading and/or discharge stipulated in the Credit,

and

iv consists of a sole original non-negotiable sea waybill, or if issued in more than one original, the full set as so issued,
and

v appears to contain all of the terms and conditions of carriage, or some of such terms and conditions by reference to a source or document other than the non-negotiable sea waybill (short form/blank back non-negotiable sea waybill); banks will not examine the contents of such terms and conditions,
and

vi   contains no indication that it is subject to a charter party and/or no indication that the carrying vessel is propelled by sail only,

and

vii in all other respects meets the stipulations of the Credit.

b   For the purpose of this Article, transhipment means unloading and reloading from one vessel to another vessel during the course of ocean carriage from the port of loading to the port of discharge stipulated in the Credit.

c   Unless transhipment is prohibited by the terms of the Credit, banks will accept a non-negotiable sea waybill which indicates that the goods will be transhipped, provided that the entire ocean carrier is covered by one and the same non-negotiable sea waybill.

d   Even if the Credit prohibits transhipment, banks will accept a non-negotiate sea waybill which:

i   indicates that transhipment will take place as long as the relevant cargo is shipped in Container(s), Trailer(s) and/or "LASH" barge(s) as evidenced by the non-negotiable sea waybill, provided that the entire ocean carriage is covered by one and the same non-negotiable sea waybill,

and/or

ii incorporates clauses stating that the carrier reserves the right to tranship.

Article 25 - <u>Charter Party Bill of Lading</u>

a   If a Credit calls for or permits a charter party bill of lading, banks will, unless otherwise stipulated in the Credit, accept a document, however named, which:

i   contains any indication that it is subject to a charter party,

and

ll appears on its face to have been signed or otherwise authenticated by:

- the master or a named agent for or on behalf of the master, or

- the owner or a named agent for or on behalf of the owner. Any signature or authentication of the master or owner must be identified as master or owner as the case may be . An agent signing or authenticating for the master or owner must also indicate the name and the capacity of the party, i.e. master or owner, on whose behalf that agent is acting.

and

iii does or does not indicate the name of the carrier,

and

iv indicates that the goods have been loaded on board or shipped on a named vessel.

Loading on board or shipment on a named vessel may be indicated by pre-printed wording on the bill of lading that the goods have been loaded on board a named vessel or shipped on a named vessel, in which case the date of issuance of the bill of lading will be deemed to the date of loading on board and the date of shipment.

In all other cases loading on board a named vessel must be evidenced by a notation on the bill of lading which gives the date on which the goods have been loaded on board, in which case the date of the on board notation will be deemed to be the date of shipment,

and

v indicates the port of loading and the port of discharge stipulated in the Credit,

and

vi consists of a sole original bill of lading or, if issued in more than one original, the full set as so issued,

and

vii contains no indication that the carrying vessel is propelled by sail only,

and

viii in all other respects meets the stipulations of the Credit.

b Even if the Credit requires the presentation of a charter party contract in connection with a charter party bill of lading, banks will not examine such charter party contract, but will pass it on without responsibility on their part.

Article 26 - <u>Multimodal Transport Document</u>

a   If a Credit calls for a transport document covering at least two different modes of transport (multimodal transport), banks will, unless otherwise stipulated in the Credit, accept a document, however named, which:

i   appears on its face to indicate the name of the carrier or multimodal transport operator and to have been signed or otherwise authenticated by:

   • the carrier or multimodal transport operator or a named agent for or on behalf of the carrier or multimodal transport operator, or
   • the master or a named agent for or on behalf of the master.

Any signature or authentication of the carrier, multimodal transport operator or master must be identified as carrier, multimodal transport operator or master, as the case may be. An agent signing or authenticating for the carrier, multimodal transport operator or master must also indicate the name and the capacity of the party, i.e., carrier, multimodal transport operator or master, on whose behalf the agent is acting.

ii   indicates that the goods have been dispatched, taken in charge or loaded on board.

Dispatch, taking in charge or loading on board may be indicated by wording to that effect on the multimodal transport document and the date of issuance will be deemed to be the date of dispatch, taking in charge or loading on board and the date of shipment. However, if the document indicates, by stamp or otherwise, a date of dispatch, taking in charge or loading on board, such date will be deemed to be the date of shipment, and

iii   a   indicates the place of taking in charge stipulated in the Credit which may be different from the port, airport or place of loading, and the place of final destination stipulated in the Credit which may be different from the port, airport or place of discharge, and/or

b contains the indication "intended" or similar qualification in relation to the vessel and/or port of loading and/or port of discharge,

and

iv consists of a sole original multimodal transport document or, if issued in more than one original, the full set as so issued, and

v appears to contain all of the terms and conditions of carriage, or some of such terms and conditions by reference to a source or document other than the multimodal transport document (short form/blank back multimodal transport document); banks will not examine the contents of such terms and conditions,

and

vi contains no indication that it is subject to a charter party and/or no indication that the carrying vessel is propelled by sail only,

and

vii in all other respects meets the stipulations of the Credit.

b Even if the Credit prohibits transhipment, banks will accept a multimodal transport document which indicates that transhipment will or may take place, provided that the entire carriage is covered by one and the same multimodal transport document.

Article 27 - Air Transport Document

a If a Credit calls for an air transport document banks will, unless otherwise stipulated in the Credit, accept a document, however named, which:

i appears on its face to indicate the name of the carrier and to have been signed or otherwise authenticated by:
  • the carrier, or
  • a named agent for or on behalf of the carrier.

Any signature or authentication of the carrier must be identified as carrier. An agent signing or authenticating for the carrier must also indicate the name and the capacity of the party, i.e. carrier, on whose behalf that agent is acting,

and

ii indicates that the goods have been accepted for carriage,

and

iii where the Credit calls for an actual date of dispatch, indicates a specific notation of such date, the date of dispatch so indicated on the air transport document will be deemed to be the date of shipment.

For the purpose of this Article, the information appearing in the box on the air transport document (marked "For Carrier Use Only" or similar expression) relative to the flight number and date will be considered as a specific notation of such date of dispatch.

In all other cases, the date of issuance of the air transport document will be deemed to be the date of shipment,

and

iv indicates the airport of departure and the airport of destination stipulated in the Credit,

and

v appears to be the original for consignor/shipper even if the Credit stipulates a full set of originals, or similar expressions,

and

vi appears to contain all of the terms and conditions of carriage, or some of such terms and conditions, by reference to a source or document other than the air transport document; banks will not examine the contents of such terms and conditions,

and

vii in all other respects meets the stipulations of the Credit.

b   For the purpose of this Article, transhipment means unloading and reloading from one aircraft to another aircraft during the course of carriage from the airport of departure to the airport of destination stipulated in the Credit.

c   Even if the Credit prohibits transhipment, banks will accept an air transport document which indicates that transhipment will or may take place, provided that the entire carriage is covered by one and the same air transport document.

Article 28 - Road, Rail or Inland Waterway Transport Documents

a   If a Credit calls for a road, rail, or inland waterway transport document, banks will, unless otherwise stipulated in the Credit, accept a document of the type called for, however named, which:
i   appears on its face to indicate the name of the carrier and to have been signed or otherwise authenticated by the carrier or a named agent for or on behalf of the carrier and/or to bear a reception stamp or other indication of receipt by the carrier or a named agent for or on behalf of the carrier.
Any signature, authentication, reception stamp or other indication of receipt of the carrier, must be identified on its face as that of the carrier. An agent signing or authenticating for the carrier must also indicate the name and the capacity of the party, i.e. carrier, on whose behalf that agent is acting,
and
ii   indicates that the goods have been received for shipment, dispatch or carriage or wording to this effect. The date of issuance will be deemed to be the date of shipment unless the transport document contains a reception stamp, in which case the date of the reception stamp will be deemed to be the date of shipment,
and
iii   indicates the place of shipment and the place of destination stipulated in the Credit,
and
iv   in all other respects meets the stipulations of the Credit.

b   In the absence of any indication on the transport document as to the numbers issued, banks will accept the transport document(s) presented as constituting a full set. Banks will accept as original(s) the transport document(s) whether marked as original(s) or not.

c   For the purpose of this Article, transhipment means unloading
and reloading from one means of conveyance to another means
of conveyance, in different modes of transport, during the course
of carriage from the place of shipment to the place of destination stipulated in the Credit.

d   Even if the Credit prohibits transhipments, banks will accept a
road, rail, or inland waterway transport document which indicates that transhipment will or may take place, provided that
the entire carriage is covered by one and the same transport
document and within the same mode or transport.

Article 29 - <u>Courier and Post Receipts</u>

a   If a Credit calls for a post receipt or certificate of posting, banks
will, unless otherwise stipulated in the Credit, accept a post receipt or certificate of posting which:
i   appears on its face to have been stamped or otherwise authenticated and dated in the place from which the Credit stipulates the goods are to be shipped or dispatched and such date
will be deemed to be the date of shipment or dispatch,
and
ii   in all other respects meets the stipulations of the Credit.

b   If a Credit calls for a document issued by a courier or expedited
delivery service evidencing receipt of the goods for delivery, banks
will, unless otherwise stipulated in the Credit, accept a document, however named, which:
i   appears on its face to indicate the name of the courier/serv-
ice, and to have been stamped, signed or otherwise authenticated by such named courier/service (unless the Credit specifically calls for a document issued by a named Courier/Service,
banks will accept a document issued by any Courier/Service),
and
ii   indicates a date of pick up or of receipt or wording to this
effect, such date being deemed to be the date of shipment or
dispatch,

and

iii in all other respects meets the stipulations of the Credit.

Article 30 - <u>Transport Documents Issued by Freight Forwarders</u>

Unless otherwise authorized in the Credit, banks will only accept a transport document issued by a freight forwarder if it appears on its face to indicate:

i the name of the freight forwarder as a carrier or multimodal transport operator and to have been signed or otherwise authenticated by the freight forwarder as carrier or multimodal transport operator,

or

ii the name of the carrier or multimodal transport operator and to have been signed or otherwise authenticated by the freight forwarder as a named agent for or on behalf of the carrier or multimodal transport operator.

Article 31 - <u>"On Deck", "Shipper's Load and Count", Name of Consignor</u>

Unless otherwise stipulated in the Credit, banks will accept a transport document which:

i does not indicate, in the case of carriage by sea or by more than one means of conveyance including carriage by sea, that the goods are or will be loaded on deck. Nevertheless, banks will accept a transport document which contains a provision that the goods may be carried on deck, provided that it does not specifically state that they are or will be loaded on deck, and/or

ii bear a clause on the face thereof such as "shipper's load and count" or "said by shipper to contain" or words of similar effect, and/or

iii indicates as the consignor of the goods a party other than the Beneficiary of the Credit.

Article 32 - <u>Clean Transport Documents</u>

a   A clean transport document is one which bears no clause or notation which expressly declares a defective condition of the goods and/or the packaging.

b   Banks will not accept transport documents bearing such clauses or notations unless the Credit expressly stipulates the clauses or notations which may be accepted.

c   Banks will regard a requirement in a Credit for a transport document to bear the clause "clean on board" as complied with if such transport document meets the requirements of this Article and of Articles 23, 24, 25, 26, 27, 28 or 30.

Article 33 - <u>Freight Payable / Prepaid Transport Documents</u>

a   Unless otherwise stipulated in the Credit, or inconsistent with any of the documents presented under the Credit, banks will accept transport documents stating that freight or transportation charges (hereafter referred to as "freight") have still to be paid.

b   If a Credit stipulates that the transport document has to indicate that freight has been paid or prepaid, banks will accept a transport document on which words clearly indicating payment or prepayment of freight appear by stamp or otherwise, or on which payment or prepayment of freight is indicated by other means. If the Credit requires courier charges to be paid or prepaid, banks will also accept a transport document issued by a courier or expedited delivery service evidencing that courier charges are for the account of a party other than the consignee.

c   The words "freight prepayable" or "freight to be prepaid" or words of similar effect, if appearing on transport documents, will not be accepted as constituting evidence of the payment of freight.

d   Banks will accept transport documents bearing reference by stamp or otherwise to costs additional to the freight, such as costs of, or disbursements incurred in connection with, loading, unloading or similar operations, unless the conditions of the Credit specifically prohibit such reference.

Article 34 - Insurance Documents

a   Insurance documents must appear on their face to be issued and signed by insurance companies or underwriters or their agents.

b   If the insurance document indicates that it has been issued in more than one original, all the originals must be presented unless otherwise authorized in the Credit.

c   Cover notes issued by brokers will not be accepted, unless specifically authorized in the Credit.

d   Unless otherwise stipulated in the Credit, banks will accept an insurance certificate or a declaration under an open cover presigned by insurance companies or underwriters or their agents. If a Credit specifically calls for an insurance certificate or a declaration under an open cover, banks will accept, in lieu thereof, an insurance policy.

e   Unless otherwise stipulated in the Credit, or unless it appears from the insurance document that the cover is effective at the latest from the date of loading on board or dispatch or taking in charge of the goods, banks will not accept an insurance document which bears a date of issuance later than the date of loading on board or dispatch or taking in charge as indicated in such transport document.

f   i   Unless otherwise stipulated in the Credit, the insurance document must be expressed in the same currency as the Credit.
ii   Unless otherwise stipulated in the Credit, the minimum amount for which the insurance document must indicate the insurance cover to have been effected is the CIF (cost, insurance and freight ("named port of destination")) or CIP (carriage and insurance paid to ("named place of destination")) value of the goods, as the case may be, plus 10%, but only when the CIF or CIP value can be determined from the documents on their face. Otherwise, banks will accept as such minimum

amount 110% of the amount for which payment, acceptance or negotiation is requested under the Credit, or 110% of the gross amount of the invoice, whichever is the greater.

Article 35 - <u>Type of Insurance Cover</u>

a   Credit should stipulate the type of insurance required and, if any, the additional risks which are to be covered. Imprecise terms such as "usual risks" or "customary risks" shall not be used; if they are used, banks will accept insurance documents as presented, without responsibility for any risks not being covered.

b   Failing specific stipulations in the Credit, banks will accept insurance documents as presented, without responsibility for any risks not being covered.

c   Unless otherwise stipulated in the Credit, banks will accept an insurance document which indicates that the cover is subject to a franchise or an excess (deductible).

Article 36 - <u>All Risks Insurance Cover</u>

Where a Credit stipulates "insurance against all risks", banks will accept an insurance document which contain any "all risks" notation or clause, whether or not bearing the heading "all risks", even if the insurance document indicates that certain risks are excluded, without responsibility for any risk(s) not being covered.

Article 37 - <u>Commercial Invoices</u>

a   Unless otherwise stipulated in the Credit, commercial invoices
    i   must appear on their face to be issued by the Beneficiary named in the Credit (except as provided in Article 48),
    and
    ii   must be made out in the name of the Applicant, (except as provided in sub-Article 48 (h)),
    and
    iii   need not be signed.

b   Unless otherwise stipulated in the Credit, banks may refuse commercial invoices issued or amounts in excess of the amount permitted by the Credit. Nevertheless, if a bank authorized to pay, incur a deferred payment undertaking, accept Draft(s), or negotiate under a Credit accepts such invoices, its decision will be binding upon all parties, provided that such bank has not paid, incurred a deferred payment undertaking, accepted Draft(s) or negotiated for an amount in excess of that permitted by the Credit.

c   The description of the goods in the commercial invoice must correspond with the description in the Credit. In all other documents, the goods may be described in general terms not inconsistent with the description of the goods in the Credit.

Article 38 - Other Documents

If a Credit calls for an attestation or certification of weight in the case of transport other than by sea, banks will accept a weight stamp or declaration of weight which appears to have been superimposed on the transport document unless the Credit specifically stipulates that the attestation or certification of weight must be by means of a separate document.

E. Miscellaneous Provisions

Article 39 - Allowance in Credit Amount, Quantity and Unit Price

a   The words "about", "approximately", "circa" or similar expressions used in connection with the amount of the Credit or the quantity or the unit price stated in the Credit are to be construed as allowing a difference not to exceed 10% more or 10% less than the amount or the quantity or the unit price to which they refer.

b   Unless a Credit stipulates that the quantity of the goods specified must not be exceeded or reduced, a tolerance of 5% more or 5% less will be permissible, always provided that the amount of the drawings does not exceed the amount of the Credit. This tolerance does not apply when the Credit stipulates the quantity in terms of a stated number of packing units or individual items.

c   Unless a Credit which prohibits partial shipments stipulates otherwise, or unless sub-Article (b) above is applicable, a tolerance of 5% less in the amount of the drawing will be permissible, provided that if the Credit stipulates the quantity of the goods, such quantity of goods is shipped in full, and if the Credit stipulates a unit price, such price is not reduced. This provision does not apply when expressions referred to in sub-Article (a) above are used in the Credit.

Article 40 - Partial Shipments/Drawings

a   Partial drawings and/or shipments are allowed, unless the Credit stipulates otherwise.

b   Transport documents which appear on their face to indicate that shipment has been made on the same means of conveyance and for the same journey, provided they indicate the same destination, will not be regarded as covering partial shipments, even if the transport documents indicate different dates of shipment and/or different ports of loading, places of taking in charge, or despatch.

c   Shipment made by post or by courier will not be regarded as partial shipments if the post receipts or certificates of posting or courier's receipts or dispatch notes appear to have been stamped, signed or otherwise authenticated in the place from which the credit stipulates the goods are to be dispatched, and on the same date.

Article 41 - Instalment Shipments/Drawings

If drawings and/or shipments by instalments within given periods are stipulated in the Credit and any instalment is not drawn and/or shipped within the period allowed for that instalment, the Credit ceases to be available for that and any subsequent instalments, unless otherwise stipulated in the Credit.

Article 42 - Expiry Date and Place for Presentation of Documents

a   All Credits must stipulate an expiry date and a place for presentation of documents for payment, acceptance, or with the exception of freely negotiable Credits, a place for presentation of documents for negotiation. An expiry date stipulated for payment, acceptance or negotiation will be construed to express an expiry date for presentation of documents.

b   Except as provided in sub-Article 44(a), documents must be presented on or before such expiry date.

c   If an Issuing Bank states that the Credit is to be available "for one month", "for six months", or the like, but does not specify the date from which the time is to run, the date of issuance of the Credit by the Issuing Bank will be deemed to be the first day from which such time is to run. Banks should discourage indication of the expiry date of the Credit in this manner.

Article 43 - Limitation on the Expiry Date

a   In addition to stipulating an expiry date for presentation of documents, every Credit which calls for a transport document(s) should also stipulate a specified period of time after the date of shipment during which presentation must be made in compliance with the terms and conditions of the Credit. If no such period of time is stipulated, banks will not accept documents presented to them later than 21 days after the date of shipment. In any event, documents must be presented not later than the expiry date of the Credit.

b   In cases in which sub-Article 40(b) applies, the date of shipment will be considered to be the latest shipment date on any of the transport documents presented.

Article 44 - Extension of Expiry Date

a   If the expiry date of the Credit and/or the last day of the period of time for presentation of documents stipulated by the Credit or applicable by virtue of Article 43 falls on a day on which the bank to which presentation has to be made is closed for reasons other than those referred to in Article 17, the stipulated expiry date and/or the last day of the period of time after the date of shipment for presentation of documents, as the case may be, shall be extended to the first following day on which such bank is open.

b   The latest date for shipment shall not be extended by reason of the extension of the expiry date and/or the period of time after the date of shipment for presentation of documents in accordance with sub-Article (a) above. If no such latest date for shipment is stipulated in the Credit or amendments thereto, banks will not accept transport documents indicating a date of shipment later than the expiry date stipulated in the Credit or amendments thereto.

c   The bank to which presentation is made on such first following business day must provide a statement that the documents were presented within the time limits extended in accordance with sub-Article 44(a) of the Uniform Customs and Practice for Documentary Credits, 1993 Revision, ICC Publication No.500.

Article 45 - Hours of Presentation

Banks are under no obligation to accept presentation of documents outside their banking hours.

Article 46 - General Expressions as to Dates for Shipment

a   Unless otherwise stipulated in the Credit, the expression "shipment" used in stipulating an earliest and/or a latest date for shipment will be understood to include expressions such as, "loading on board", "dispatch", "accepted for carriage", "date of post receipt", "date of pick-up", and the like, and in the case of a Credit calling for a multimodal transport document the expression "taking in charge".

b   Expressions such as "prompt", "immediately", "as soon as possible", and the like should not be used. If they are used banks will disregard them.

c   If the expression "on or about" or similar expressions are used, banks will interpret them as a stipulation that shipment is to be made during the period from five days before to five days after the specified date, both end days included.

Article 47 - Date Terminology for Periods of Shipment

a   The words "to", "until", "till", "from" and words of similar import applying to any date or period in the Credit referring to shipment will be understood to include the date mentioned.

b   The word "after" will be understood to exclude the date mentioned.

c   The terms "first half", "second half" of a month shall be construed respectively as the 1st to the 15th, and the 16th to the last day of such month, all dates inclusive.

d   The terms "beginning", "middle", or "end" of a month shall be construed respectively as the 1st to the 10th, the 11th to the 20th, and the 21st to the last day of such month, all dates inclusive.

F. Transferable Credit

Article 48 - Transferable Credit

a   A transferable Credit is a Credit under which the Beneficiary (First Beneficiary) may request the bank authorized to pay, incur a deferred payment undertaking, accept or negotiate (the "Transferring Bank"), or in the case of a freely negotiable Credit, the bank specifically authorized in the Credit as a Transferring Bank, to make the Credit available in whole or in part to one or more than Beneficiary(ies) (Second Beneficiary(ies)).

b   A Credit can be transferred only if it is expressly designated as "transferable" by the Issuing Bank. Terms such as "divisible", "fractionable", "assignable", and "transmissible" do not render the Credit transferable. If such terms are used they shall be disregarded.

c   The Transferring Bank shall be under no obligation to effect such transfer except to the extent and in the manner expressly consented to by such bank.

d   At the time of making a request for transfer and prior to transfer of the Credit the First Beneficiary must irrevocably instruct the Transferring Bank whether or not he retains the right to refuse to allow the Transferring Bank to advise amendments to the Second Beneficiary(ies). If the Transferring Bank consent to the transfer under these conditions, it must, at the time of transfer, advise the Second Beneficiary(ies) of the First Beneficiary's instructions regarding amendments.

e   If a Credit is transferred to more than one Second Beneficiary(ies), refusal of an amendment by one or more Second Beneficiary(ies) does not invalidate the acceptance(s) by the other Second Beneficiary(ies) with respect to whom the Credit will be amended accordingly. With respect to the Second Beneficiary(ies) who rejected the amendment the Credit will remain unamended.

f   Transferring Bank charges in respect of transfers including commissions, fees, costs or expenses are payable by the First Beneficiary, unless otherwise agreed. If the Transferring Bank agrees to transfer the Credit it shall be under no obligation to effect the transfer until such charges are paid.

g   Unless otherwise stated in the Credit, a transferable Credit can be transferred once only. Consequently, the Credit cannot be transferred at the request of the Second Beneficiary to any subsequent Third Beneficiary. For the purpose of this Article, a retransfer to the First Beneficiary does not constitute a prohibited transfer.

Fractions of a transferable Credit (not exceeding in the aggregate the amount of the Credit) can be transferred separately, provided partial shipments/drawings are not prohibited, and the aggregate of such transfers will be considered as constituting only one transfer of the Credit.

h   The Credit can be transferred only on the terms and conditions specified in the original Credit, with the exception of
  - the amount of the Credit,
  - any unit price stated therein,
  - the expiry date,
  - the last date for presentation of documents in accordance with Article 43,
  - the period for shipment,

any or all of which may be reduced or curtailed.

The percentage for which insurance cover must be effected may be increased in such a way as to provide the amount of cover stipulated in the original Credit, or these Articles.

In addition, the name of the First Beneficiary can be substituted for that of the Applicant, but if the name of the Applicant is specifically required by the original Credit to appear in any document(s) other than the invoice, such requirement must be fulfilled.

i   The First Beneficiary has the right to substitute his own invoice(s) (and Draft(s)) for those of the Second Beneficiary(ies), for amounts not in excess of the original amount stipulated in the Credit and for the original unit prices if stipulated in the Credit, and upon such substitution of invoice(s) (and Draft(s)) the First Beneficiary can draw under the Credit for the difference, if any, between his invoice(s) and the Second Beneficiary's(ies') invoice(s).

When a Credit has been transferred and the First Beneficiary is to supply his own invoice(s) (and Draft(s)) in exchange for the Second Beneficiary's(ies') invoice(s) (and Draft(s)) but fails to do so on first demand, the Transferring Bank has the right to deliver to the Issuing Bank the documents received under the transferred Credit, including the Second Beneficiary's(ies') invoice(s) (and Draft(s)) without further responsibility to the First Beneficiary.

j   The First Beneficiary may request that payment or negotiation be effected to the Second Beneficiary(ies) at the place to which the Credit has been transferred up to and including the expiry date of the Credit, unless the original Credit expressly states that it may not be made available for payment or negotiation at a place other than that stipulated in the Credit. This is without prejudice to the First Beneficiary's right to substitute subsequently his own invoice(s) (and Draft(s)) for those of the Second Beneficiary(ies) and to claim any difference due to him.

G. Assignment of Proceeds

Article 49 - Assignment of Proceeds

The fact that a Credit is not stated to be transferable shall not affect the Beneficiary's right to assign any proceeds to which he may be, or may become, entitled under such Credit, in accordance with the provisions of the applicable law. This Article relates only to the assignment of proceeds and not to the assignment of the right to perform under the Credit itself.

Uniform Customs and Practice for Documentary Credits - 1993 Revision Publication No. 500 - ISBM 92.842.1155.7 (E) Published in is official English version by the International Chamber of Commerce Copyright 1990 - International Chamber of Commerce (ICC), Paris Available from : ICC Publishing S.A., 38 Cours Albert ler, 75008 Paris, France or from : Canadian Council for International Business, Delta Office Tower, 501-350 Sparks Street, Ottawa, Ontario, K1R 7S8, Canada.

Chapter VIII

GLOSSARY OF TECHNICAL TERMS

On the following pages you will find expressions which are frequently used in connection with documentary credits. A short explanation of the technical terms will illustrate their meaning and area of application.

About

In connection with documentary credits "about" means a tolerance of plus/minus 10% regarding the documentary credit value, unit price, or the quantity of the goods, depending on the context in which the tolerance is mentioned. See UCPDC Art.39a.

Acceptance

Acceptance of a bill of exchange occurs when the drawee commits himself to pay by putting his signature on the bill of exchange. The drawee's signature alone is a valid acceptance and is usually made across the left margin of the bill of exchange.

Acceptance Letter of Credit

Documentary credits which, in addition to the other documents, require presentation of a term draft drawn on the bank nominated as the accepting bank under the documentary credit. See UCPDC Art.9iii, and biii.

Advance Payment Guarantee

Under normal circumstances submitted by the seller's bank in the form of an obligation to pay (guarantee). Serves as a guarantee against any claims by the purchaser versus the seller for reimbursement of a downpayment made by the former prior to delivery of the goods. The right to reimbursement of the downpayment arises in the event of non-delivery of the goods or delivery which is not in compliance with the contract.

Advances

In the case of documentary credits available by deferred payment the beneficiary of the documentary credit may, under certain circumstances, be able to obtain payment at sight from the advising/issuing bank subject to the deduction of interest calculated at the usual (market) rate. The purchaser is not debited for the value of the documents until the maturity date.

Advise/advising bank

Forwarding of a documentary credit received from the issuing bank to the beneficiary (seller). For information on the responsibilities of the advising bank see UCPDC Art.7 and 12.

Air waybill

Transport document issued for carriage by air in the form of confirmation of acceptance of goods for carriage. Not a negotiable instrument. The conditions of carriage are uniformly laid down in the Warsaw Agreement of 12.10.1929 and the subsequent additional protocols.
House air waybills are also common (see explanation under this term). See UCPDC Art.27.

All risks

Insurance "against risks." This clause is often specified in documentary credits. Bank's accept insurance documents in which this clause appears even if the same document excludes coverage of certain risks. See UCPDC Art.36.

Amendments (to documentary credits)

Amendment of the current documentary credit conditions (e.g. extension of the documentary credit's validity period, shipping deadline, etc.) as given by the issuing bank on instructions from the purchaser. If irrevocable documentary credits are to the amended, all parties involved must be in agreement in order that the amendments be valid. See UCPDC Art.9d.
Concerning revocable documentary credits please refer to UCPDC Art.8.

Approval basis

If documents containing discrepancies are presented to the nominated bank under a documentary credit, the bank can forward the documents to the issuing bank for approval, with the beneficiary's agreement. Because of the risk of loss in transit and delays resulting in interest loss, however, it is recommended that the beneficiary first tries to correct the documents but, if that is not possible, asks the nominated bank to contact the issuing bank for authorization to accept the discrepancies.

Approximately

See explanation under "About."

Assignment under the documentary credit

The beneficiary of a documentary credit is entitled to assign his/her claims to any of the proceeds that he/she may by entitled to, or portions thereof, to a third party. See UCPDC Art.49.

Usually the beneficiary informs the issuing or advising bank that his/her claims or partial claims under the documentary credit were assigned and asks the bank to advise the assignee (third party) that it has acknowledged the assignment.

The assignment of proceeds under the documentary credit as described here is to be distinguished from the transfer of the documentary credit pursuant to UCPDC Art 48.

The validity of the assignment is not dependent on the bank's approval. In contrast, the transfer requires the agreement of the nominated bank. An assignment is possible regardless of whether the documentary credit is transferable.

Availability under documentary credits

Documentary credits must indicate how they are available, i.e.:

a)   by sight payment: payment on receipt of the documents by the issuing bank, or the bank nominated in the documentary credit.

b)   by deferred payment: payment after a period specified in the documentary credit, often calculated as number of days after the date of presentation of the documents or after the shipping date.

c)   by acceptance: acceptance of a draft (to be presented together with other documents) by the issuing bank or by the bank nominated in the documentary credit, and the payment thereof at maturity.

d)   by negotiation: meaning the giving of value by the nominated bank to the beneficiary for the documents presented, subject to receipt of cover from the issuing bank. See also UCPDC Art.9. See also remarks under "Risk of loss in transit" (place of availability).

Aval

See under "joint and several guarantee."

Back-to-back documentary credit

The back-to-back documentary credit is not a type of documentary credit specifically covered under the UCPDC. It is a separate documentary credit which is opened on the basis of and on the same terms as an already existing (original) credit, i.e. back-to-back (See Figure 8.1).

Figure 8.1: Back-to-Back Documentary Credit

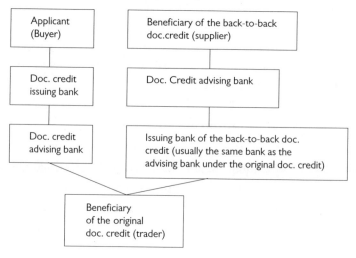

Bank guarantees

Unilateral contract between a bank as guarantor and a beneficiary warrantee in which the bank commits itself versus the beneficiary to pay a certain sum if a third party fails to perform or if any other specified event resulting in a default fails to take place.

Bill of exchange

See explanation under "Draft."

Bill of lading (B/L)

A transport document signed by the ship's master or his agent, or by the carrier or its agent, which is considered a title document. Confirms receipt of the goods and the conditions under which carriage was carried out. Release of the goods at the stipulated port of destination takes place only against presentation and handing over of a correctly endorsed original of the bill of lading.
See UCPDC Art.23, 25 and sample in Chapter 6.

Cancellation of documentary credits

See explanation under "Amendments (to documentary credits)." See UCPDC Art.9d.

Carrier

Company whose business is the transport of goods. The carrier is usually liable for the whole transport route he covers, regardless of whether the goods are carried by his own and/or other means of transport. The UCPDC requires that most transport documents are issued by the carrier or his agent or by the captain/master or his agents. See UCPDC Art.23 to 28.

Certificate of inspection

Document specifying that the goods were inspected prior to shipment. Usually issued by a neutral party.

Certificate

Certificate of any kind will usually require the signature (See explanation under "Signatures on documents") of the issuer (e.g. certificates of quality, insurance certificates, etc.). See UCPDC Art.20d.

Certification/legalization

Official certification of the authenticity of signatures or documents in connection with documentary credits, such as certificates of origin, commercial invoices, etc. by chambers of commerce, consulates, and similar recognized government authorities.

Charter Party Contract (B/L)

Contract according to which the precisely designated freight room of a ship or the whole ship is leased by the owner to a charter for a specific period or a specific journey. If a ship is chartered without crew this is a bare boat charter. The freight documents issued by the current charter or his authorized party are called "charter party B/L." See UCPDC Art.25 and sample in Chapter 6.

CIM

An internationally standardized freight document issued in rail transport. CIM stands for "Convention Internationale concernant le transport des Marchandises par chemin de fer." The agreement has been in force since 1.1.1965 and constitutes the legal basis for the conclusion of freight contracts in international rail goods transport with one and the same freight documents. See UCPDC Art.28 .

Claused bill of lading

Claused on bills of lading which note the deficient condition of the goods and/or the packaging.
See UCPDC Art.32 and brochure "Clean Transport Documents" No.473 of the International Chamber of Commerce in Paris.

Clean bill of lading

Bill of lading which does not contain clauses or notations declaring a defective condition of the goods and/or the packaging. See UCPDC Art.32 and brochure "Clean Transport Documents," No.473 of the International Chamber of Commerce in Paris.

CMR

Abbreviation for "Convention relative au contrat de transport international de Marchandises par Route." Transport document issued for shipment by road (Road waybill). See UCPDC Art.28.

Combined (transport) bill of lading/Combined transport document

Document for combined transport which covers at least two different modes of transport. As of recently the term "Multimodal Transport Document" is increasingly being used. See UCPDC Arc.26.

Commercial invoice

Invoice of the supplier which refers to the goods delivered or the service carried out for the purchaser. The description of the goods or service in the invoice must match exactly that in the documentary credit. In all other documents the goods or service description may be made in general terms, not inconsistent with the description of the goods in the credit. Incoterms, etc. stated in the documentary credit are to be noted in the commercial invoice. See UCPDC Art.37 and sample in Chapter 6.

Commissions

As a rule documentary credits should indicate whether bank commissions are charged to the applicant (purchaser) or the beneficiary (seller). If this information is not contained in the documentary credit, the applicant (purchaser) bears all the bank commissions. This also applies to charges of the reimbursing bank. See UCPDC Art.18c.

Commitment

Under certain conditions banks commit themselves to confirm export letters of credit which their customers expect to be issued. Generally such commitments would be given for a certain period of time. The exporter is billed for an agreed commitment commission for the period from the issuance of the commitment letter until the receipt of the corresponding documentary credit.

Commodity trade finance

Transactional financing in which a credit line is agreed between the trading company and the bank. The type of security is usually linked to the transaction to be financed. The risk evaluation is based on the financial condition of the trading company, on the one hand, and the supplier/performance risk, on the other.

Conference line

Ocean shipping companies whose ships travel according to firmly established schedules along fixed routes. Uniform transport rates are established between the shipping lines.
Such agreements are usually called conferences. The conference lines are therefore the shipping routes agreed by the conferences.

Confirmation (of documentary credits)

In addition to the commitment of the issuing bank the advising bank makes its own, independent payment commitment when it adds its confirmation. See under UCPDC Art.9b.
Confirmation will only be added to irrevocable documentary credits, usually available with the advising bank. If confirmation of the documentary credit is desired, the applicant must state this expressly in his/her documentary credit application. The confirming bank assumes the credit risk of the issuing bank as well as the political and transfer risks of the purchaser's country. See under these three terms. If a documentary credit does not contain a confirmation request by the issuing bank, in certain circumstances the possibility exists of confirming the documentary credit "by silent confirmation," i.e. with-

out the issuing bank's knowledge.
Without confirmation of the documentary credit, the advising bank
will forward the documentary credit to the beneficiary without taking on its own commitment.

Confirmed reimbursement undertaking

Confirmation by the reimbursement bank to the bank authorized to
pay, accept, or negotiate, that the former will honor the latter's requests for reimbursements under the documentary credit. The reimbursing bank thus makes a commitment to pay.

Consignment note

The consignment note is often understood to mean the CMR (explanation see under "CMR") in the case of documentary credits. The
transport documents to be presented should, however, be precisely
stated, as other documents such as the railway bill, etc. could otherwise be considered to be valid.

Consignor (Shipper)

The consignor is understood to be the party who delivers the goods
in his/her own name to the carrier (e.g., shipowner) based on a freight
contract. The shipper will usually be either the exporter or his/her
forwarder. The shipper is usually also the party in whose name the
shipment is carried out and who appears as the consignor in the transport document.

Consolidator

Forwarder who gathers mixed cargo in order to better utilize the space
in transport containers.

Container

In documentary operations, loading into containers is relevant to the
extent that this may be taken into account when examining documents. Example: Even if a documentary credit prohibits transhipment banks will accept bills of lading/sea waybills which indicate

transhipment, provided that the goods were shipped in container, trailers, or LASH barges (lighter aboard ship) and that the whole ocean carriage is covered by one and the same bill of lading/sea way-bill. See UCPDC Art.23 d, 24 d.

Copies

If documentary credits call for copies of documents, banks will accept documents which are either marked as copies or not marked as originals. See UCPDC Art.20 c i.

If documentary credits call for multiple documents (e.g. three copies), banks will accept one original, and the remaining number in copies unless the document itself indicates otherwise. See UCPDC Art.20 c ii.

Correction of documents (in connection with documentary credits)

The beneficiary of a documentary credit has the right to correct or replace documents found to contain discrepancies by the nominated bank within the period of validity of the documentary credit, or within the period for presentation and to present the documents to the nominated bank again. Corrections to documents may be made only by the issuer or a party authorized by the issuer. In each case the document must clearly show who made the correction.

In the case of legalized documents the corrections themselves must also be legalized again.

Cover Note

Often also called "broker's cover note." Document issued by insurance companies or insurance brokers in lieu of insurance policies or insurance certificates which serves as proof of usual insurance notification and represents cover approval. Cover notes may be accepted under documentary credits only when they are expressly permitted. See UCPDC Art.34 c.

Credit risk

This risk includes both the inability to pay and the unwillingness to pay of a debtor. Through the opening of a documentary credit the issuing bank takes over the purchaser's liability for performance. For the seller the credit risk is therefore with the issuing bank. If a documentary credit is confirmed by the advising bank, the latter assumes the liability towards the beneficiary. In this way both the credit risk of the issuing bank and the country risk (transfer and political risks) of the same are excluded for the beneficiary.

Deadline for examining documents (by the bank)

The banks are allowed a reasonable time to examine the documents presented under the credit, such reasonable time not to exceed 7 bank working days following the day of receipt of the documents. See UCPDC Arc.13 b.

Description of goods

The description of the goods in the commercial invoice must correspond exactly to that in the documentary credit. In all other documents it may be expressed in general terms, not inconsistent with the description of the goods in the documentary credit. See UCPDC Art.37 c.

Discounting

The beneficiary under a usance/term documentary credit has the possibility of the discounting his claim. The bank credits the beneficiary with the value of the documents, less the discount, but on an unconfirmed credit, reserves the right of recourse (explanation see under "Recourse"). In the case of a confirmed documentary credit the discount would be without recourse.

Discrepancies (in the documents)

Information (or missing information or missing documents/papers, etc.) in the documents submitted under a documentary credit, which

- is not consistent with its terms and conditions

- is inconsistent with other documents submitted
- does not meet the requirements of the Uniform Customs and Practice for Documentary Credits (UCPDC), brochure no.522, 1995 revision.

If the documents show discrepancies of any kind, the issuing bank is no longer obliged to pay and, in the case of a confirmed documentary credit, neither is the confirming bank (strict documentary compliance). See UCPDC Art.14.

Documentary collection

A documentary collection is the instruction of the seller to his bank to collect the value of the documents from the purchaser by handing over the documents against payment or an undertaking to pay. In this context the instructions relating to the payment terms may state either "documents against payment" or "documents against acceptance of a draft." The bank acts as a fiduciary and makes every effort to ensure that payment is received. In contrast to the documentary credit, in the case of documentary collections the banks are liable only for the correct execution of the collection instructions, and do not make any commitment to pay themselves. Documentary collections are subject to the regulations of the Uniform Rules for Collections, Brochure No. 322, revised 1978, of the International Chamber of Commerce in Paris.

Documentary credit (definition)

A documentary credit is
1. the written assurance of a bank
2. on the instructions of the applicant (purchaser)
3. to the beneficiary (seller)
4. to pay a specific amount
5. in the agreed currency provided the beneficiary
6. submits documents in conformity with the documentary credit
7. within the prescribed deadlines

See Figure 8.2. See UCPDC Art.2.

Figure 8.2: Documentary Credit Sample

❶ Federal Deposit Bank

MT700 ISSUANCE OF L/C   ***   BEGINNING OF MESSAGE

The following pages are an integral part of the L/C. Except if otherwise stipulated, this L/C is subject to the Union Customs and Practice for Documentary Credits, International Chamber of Commerce, Paris, as in effect on the date of issuance of the L/C is freely negotiable, each utilization must be noted on the reverse of this advice by the negotiation ban.

27	SEQUENCE TOTAL OF SEQUENCE	I / I
40A	FORM OF L/C	IRREVOCABLE
20	OUR REFERENCE	DOC-10-IQ.00812
31C	DATE OF ISSUE	03.11.97
31D	DATE AND PLACE OF EXPIRY	
❼	21.12.97 / NEW YORK	
50	APPLICANT	
❷	KORSHUN CORPORATION	
	TORONTO CANADA	
59	BENEFICIARY	
❸	KATION INC.	
	NEW YORK	
32B	CURRENCY AND AMOUNT	
❺	USD ❹ 160,000	
41D	AVAILABLE WITH / BY BY PAYMENT	
	FEDERAL DEPOSIT BANK	
43P	PARTIAL DRAWINGS / SHIPMENTS	
	PERMITTED	
43T	TRANSHIPMENT	
	PROHIBITED	
44A	DISPATCH FROM/BY	
	NEW YORK BY SEA	
44B	FOR TRANSPORTATION TO	
	HAMBURG	
44C	LATEST DATE OF SHIPMENT	
	7 30.11.97	

45AB DESCRIPTION OF GOODS AND/OR SERVICES
   FOB NEW YORK
   4 AUTOMOBILES AS PER CONTRACT A7956.1
46AB DOCUMENTS REQUIRED
❻   +SIGNED COMMERCIAL INVOICE 3-FOLD
   +PACKING LIST
   +CERTIFICATE OF ORIGIN
   +FULL SET (3/3) ORIGINAL GLEAN ON BOARD OCEAN BILLS OF
   LADING MADE OUT TO ORDER AND BLANK ENDORSED
NOTIFYING NEW FORWARDING LTD. AND MARKED FREIGHT COLLECT
47AB ADDITIONAL CONDITIONS
   A FEE OF CHF 100.00 (OR EQUIVALENT) WILL BE DEDUCTED
   FROM THE PROCEEDS FOR EACH SET OF DOCUMENTS PRESENTED
   WITH DISCREPANCIES. CONSECUTIVE COVERS, BY REGISTERED AIRMAIL.

```
71B  COMMISSIONS / CHARGES
     ALL COMMISSIONS AND CHARGES OUTSIDE
     NEW YORK ARE FOR BENEFICIARY'S ACCOUNT
48   PERIOD FOR PRESENTATION OF DOCUMENTS
     WITHIN 21 DAYS AFTER THE DATE OF ISSUANCE OF THE TRANS PORT
     DOCUMENTS.
49   CONFIRMATION INSTRUCTIONS
     WITHOUT
72   INFORMATION TO ADVISING BANK
     UPON RECEIPT AND VERIFICATION OF STRICTLY CREDIT CONFORM
     DOCUMENTS AT OUR COUNTERS IN NEW YORK WE SHALL REMIT
     FUNDS AS PER YOUR INSTRUCTIONS

***  MT700   ISSUANCE OF L/C   ***   END OF MESSAGE
```

Documents

Commercial invoice, transport document, certificate of origin, packing list, etc. required under a documentary credit and collection.

Draft (Bill of exchange)

Documentary credits often require presentation of a draft drawn by the beneficiary on the issuing bank, the confirming bank, or the reimbursing bank. UCPDC Art. 9 a iv. states that a credit should not be issued available by draft drawn on the applicant.

Endorsement

A notation of transfer usually on the back of a document signed by the endorser. The documentary credit frequently calls for the following documents which are transferred by endorsement:
   a) bill of exchange
   b) bill of lading
   c) insurance document

EUR 1

Goods transport certificate and proof of preference for export in countries and regions associated with the EC (and EEA) through free trade agreements, association or preferential agreements, as long as the goods concerned are included in the tariffs preferences.

Excess in connection with insurance

If, for example, an insurance certificate states that insurance is subject to a 5% excess, then 5% of the process of any claims will be deducted.

Factoring

Sales financing in which the factor purchases all the account receivables of an exporter arising from delivery of goods, minus the factoring fee and interest for the period up to the (average) due date of the receivables.

FCL (Full Container Load)

In contrast to the LCL (Less than Container Load, see explanation under "LCL") the carrier / shipowner takes an already fully loaded container for carriage from the shipper (exporter).

FCR (Forwarder's Certificate of Receipt)

Confirms that the goods have been accepted for carriage to, or held at the disposal of, the consignee. See example in Chapter 4.

FIO

Explanation see under "free in …"

Force majeure

Banks assume no liability for the consequences arising out of interruption of their business operations due to force majeure. See under UCPDC Art.17.

Forfeiting (under documentary credits)

Purchase by the bank of individual claims, payable in the future, under, among other things, documentary credits whereby the bank renounces any recourse to the seller of the debt. The bank credits the value of the documents minus the forfeiting interest.

Forwarder's documents

Transport documents issued by a forwarding company. For these to be acceptable under UCPDC, the issuer must sign the document as the carrier or as the multimodal transport operator, or as an agent of a named carrier or multimodal transport operator. See UCPDC Art. 30 and Chapter 6.

Franchise (in connection with insurances)

If, for example, an insurance certificate states that insurance is subject to a franchise of 5%, claims will only be payable if any losses exceed this figure. Insurance documents indicating a franchise are accepted under documentary credits as long as they are not expressly prohibited. See UCPDC Art. 35 c.

"Free In," "Free Out," "Free In and Out" clauses

As an integral part of the delivery terms concerning maritime freight, the definition "free in - free out" covers the acceptance of costs and the liability for the movement by a specified contract party of the designated goods transported from the pier into the booked hold of the vessel and/or vice versa. If documentary credits require this type of clause, banks examine their notations on the corresponding transport document, or on the invoice.

Freely negotiable (documentary credits)

When documentary credits are stated as "freely negotiable," the beneficiary of the documentary credit has the right to present his documents at a bank of his choice for negotiation (see explanation under this term). See UCPDC Art.10.

Freight notation

Reference on the transport document which indicates whether the freight cost were paid in advance by the shipper ("freight prepaid") or are to be paid by the consignee when the goods arrive at the destination ("freight payable at destination") ("freight collect"). In charter contracts notations such as "freight payable as per charter party," etc. are also common. See UCPDC Art. 33.

Full set

All the originals of a particular document (normally bills of lading). The number of originals is usually indicated on the document itself.

GSP Form A (Generalized Systems of Preferences certificate of origin Form A)

Certificate of origin used under preferential trade agreements with developing and newly industrialized countries.

House Air Waybill (HAWB)

In air transport business the "House Air Waybill (HAWB)" is common today. It is issued by forwarding agents for air freight consolidate shipments. The HAWB is deemed to be equivalent to the AWB in documentary operations as long as it is clear that the issuer assumes liability as the carrier or acts as the agent of the named carrier. See UCPDC Art. 27.

ICC (International Chamber of Commerce in Paris)

The ICC was founded in Atlantic City in 1919. It now encompasses associations and companies from all branches of industry. Its headquarters are located at 38, Cours Albert 1er, F-75008 Paris. As an institution of international economic self-administration, it operates through expert commissions, subcommittees, and working groups to address questions which are of importance for the international business community. These include, for example, contract and delivery clauses (Incoterms), standardization of means of payment, Uniform Rules for Collection, Uniform Customs and Practice for

Documentary Credits and Position Papers referring thereto, Uniform Rules for Demand Guarantees, arbitral jurisdiction (Rules of Conciliation and Arbitration), questions relating to such issues as competition, foreign investments, transportation.

Incoterms

International rules for the uniform interpretation of common contract clauses in export/import transactions. Issued by the International Chamber of Commerce in Paris. See Incoterms, in Chapter 1.

Insurance amount

The UCPDC specify the percentage of insurance cover required on insurance documents presented under the documentary credits. See UCPDC Art. 34 f.

Insurance document

Any type of confirmation of cover in which the rights and obligations of the insured party and the insurer are laid down.

Intended

Indication which may appear on marine/ocean bills of lading, non-negotiable sea waybills, and multimodal transport documents. Examples: "intended port of shipment Hamburg," "intended ocean vessel MV Swissahoi," "intended port of discharge Hong Kong." With this reference the carrier reserves the right to change the port of loading, the ship or the port of discharge. See UCPDC Art. 23 a ii., 24 a ii.

Irrevocable (documentary credit)

Documentary credits issued subject to UCPDC 500 are deemed to be irrevocable unless expressly marked as revocable. Irrevocable documentary credits may not be amended or cancelled without the agreement of the parties involved. See UCPDC Art. 6 and 9 d i.

Issuance date of the documents

Unless prohibited by the documentary credit, documents bearing a date of issuance prior to that of the documentary credit are acceptable. See UCPDC Art. 22.

Unless otherwise stipulated in a transport document, the date of issuance is deemed to be the date of shipment or loading on board of the goods. See UCPDC Art. 23 a ii., 24 a ii., etc.

Issuer of documents

For transport documents (UCPDC Art. 23-33), insurance documents (UCPDC Art. 34) and commercial invoices (UCPDC Art. 37) special directives apply as to who may issue them. Unless otherwise stipulated in the credit, or inconsistent with the provisions of UCPDC Art. 20a, other documents may be issued by any party. See UCPDC Art. 21.

Joint and several guarantee

Payment of the bill of exchange, which is the responsibility of the drawee, can be either completely or partially guaranteed via an aval (joint and several guarantee), where the guarantor places his/her signature on the draft either alone or with corresponding explanation "per aval" or "as guarantor." If other information is lacking, the guarantor commits him/herself on behalf of the issuer.

LASH (Lighter aboard ship)

Floatable large container (lighter) used in the combined ocean and inland waterway transport of goods. Lighters are transported on specially constructed ships. See UCPDC Art. 23 d i.

Latest date for presentation

Deadline for presenting documents under a documentary credit. If no deadline is stated in the documentary credit, the complete set of documents must be presented within 21 days of the date of issue of the transport document. Documents must, however, be presented within the validity date of the documentary credit. See UCPDC Art. 43.

LCL (Less than Container Load)

In contrast to the "Full Container Load" (see explanation under "FCL") goods too small to fill a container are loaded by the carrier at a container freight station with other compatible goods received from various exporters for delivery to the same destination.

Legalization

Certification of papers (e.g. commercial invoices and certificates of origin) by the Consulate or Embassy of the importing country, usually in the exporter's or seller's country. See UCPDC Art. 20d.

Letter of Indemnity (LOI)

(Usually as an indemnity for missing bill of lading). It serves to protect the carrier/owner financially against possible repercussions in connection with the release of goods without presentation of an original bill of lading.

A letter of indemnity is used in cases in which the goods arrive at the port of destination before the original bills of lading.

The issuance of the letter of indemnity allows the purchaser to take immediate delivery of the goods, thus saving himself time, additional demurrage, storage expenses, insurance costs, etc.

Liability of the banks involved in documentary credits

The UCPDC stipulates the obligations of the issuing and confirming banks under documentary credits. See UCPDC Art. 9.

Liner Bill of Lading

Title document, issued by or on behalf of a shipping company, covering shipment on a vessel plying a regular route against a published sailing schedule. See also under "Bill of lading."

Liner Terms

Conditions under which shipping companies transport goods. The amount payable for carriage of the goods (freight) includes the cost both for loading and discharge of the vessel.

Lloyd's Register

Register of ship classifications.

Mate's receipt (M.R.)

Declaration by a ship's officer in the name of the shipping company that certain goods have been received for shipment (and sometimes shipped on board). Not a title document. Used as an interim document until the bill of lading is issued.

Multimodal Transport

Document issued by a carrier or multimodal transport operator, covering at least two modes of transport (e.g. truck/ship, rail/air). See UCPDC Art. 26.

Negotiable instruments

The following documents are typical negotiable instruments: bills of lading, warehouse receipts (if marked negotiable), bills of exchange, etc. which may be transferred to another party by endorsement (see also under this term).

Negotiable bill of lading

Bill of lading transferred by endorsement. There are three possibilities:
- to XY & Co. or their order.
- to the order of XY & Co.
- to order, without the name of the party. In this case the bill remains to the order of the shipper until he endorses it.

These types of bills of lading are usually endorsed on the reverse (See explanation under "Endorsement").

The opposite of a negotiable bill of lading is the straight bill of lading.

Negotiation

In banking, negotiation means the sale and purchase of bills of exchange and documents. In documentary operations negotiation means the giving of value for drafts and other documents by the bank authorized to negotiate. The negotiation bank has the right of recourse to the beneficiary of the documentary credit if cover is not received from the issuing bank, unless the negotiating bank has agreed to negotiate without recourse to the beneficiary, or has confirmed the credit. See UCPDC Art. 10.

Negotiation credit

Documentary credit available by negotiation.
See explanation under "Availability under documentary credits."

Non-negotiable instruments

Non-security/title documents. Ownership of the document alone does not entitle the holder to receive the goods named therein (e.g. non-negotiable sea waybill, air waybill, forwarder's receipt, etc.)

Notify party

Name and address of a party in the transport document, usually the buyer or his agent, to be notified by the shipping company of the arrival of the goods.

NVOCC (-forwarder/-operator)(Non Vessel-Owning/Operating Common Carrier)

A carrier issuing bills of lading for carriage of goods on vessels which he neither operates nor owns.

On board

Pre-printed wording on the bill of lading which indicates that the goods have been loaded on board or shipped on a named ship. In the case of received-for-shipment bills of lading, the following four parties are authorized to add this "on board" notation:
* the carrier
* the carrier's agent
* the master of the ship
* the master's agent

See UCPDC Art. 23, 24, 25, 26.

On deck

Notation on the bill of lading which indicates that the goods have been loaded on the deck of the ship. Documents with an "on deck" notation will only be accepted if expressly authorized in the credit.

Original documents

Unless otherwise stated in the documentary credit, the requirement for an original document may also be satisfied by the presentation of documents produced or appearing to have been produced:

- reprographically
- by automated or computerized systems or
- as carbon copies

and marked as "originals" and where necessary appearing to be signed. See UCPDC Art. 20.

On their face

Banks must examine documents with reasonable care to ascertain whether or not they appear, on their face, to be in compliance with the terms or conditions of the documentary credit. See under UCPDC Art. 13.

Partial drawings/shipments (in connection with documentary credits)

Permitted unless expressly prohibited by the documentary credit. For partial shipments/drawings special regulations apply. See UCPDC Art. 40 and Art. 41.

Parties to the credit

At least the following three parties are involved in the documentary credit:

- Applicant (purchaser),
- Issuing bank (opening bank),
- Beneficiary (seller).

As a rule, however, the issuing bank will entrust a correspondent bank with the task of advising and authenticating the credit and, if applicable, with payment, acceptance, or negotiation. See under "Availability under documentary credits."

The issuing bank may also request the advising bank to add its confirmation.

Payment under reserve (in the case of discrepancies in the documents)

If the nominated bank is presented with documents containing discrepancies (explanation see under this term), it may agree upon provisional payment or negotiation with the agreement of the beneficiary. The nominated bank reserves the right of recourse against the beneficiary if the issuing bank refuses to accept the documents and to provide cover because of the discrepancies. Please note that certain documentary credits prohibit payment under reserve.

Performance bond

The beneficiary (buyer of the services and/or the goods) will claim financial restitution under the bond if the principal (supplier of the services and/or goods) fails to comply with the terms and conditions of the contract.

Political risk

Extraordinary measures of foreign countries and political events abroad which make it impossible for the debtor to comply with the contract or which lead to the loss, confiscation of or damage to goods belonging to the exporter, e.g. war, revolution, annexation, civil war which can have a detrimental effect upon the exporter.

An exporter may be able to cover this risk by utilizing confirmed letters of credit or by applying for cover from export credit agencies.

Port-to-port bill of lading

Marine/Ocean bill of lading which covers the transport of goods between two ocean ports. See UCPDC Art. 23.

Post office receipt/Certificate of dispatch

Receipt of a post office for the acceptance of a shipment for further carriage to the named consignee. See sample Chapter 6.

Pre-advice

At the request of the applicant the issuing bank may give a pre-advice of issuance and/or amendment of a documentary credit. A pre-advice is usually marked with a reference such as "Full details to follow." Unless otherwise stated, the pre-advice irrevocably commits the issuing bank to issue/amend the credit in a manner consistent with said pre-advice. See UCPDC Art. 11.

Purchase contract

Documentary credits are, by their nature, separate transactions from the purchase or other contracts on which they may be based. Banks will not be concerned with such contracts, even if they are referred to in any way in the documentary credit. See UCPDC Art. 3.

Quantity of goods in the documentary credit

Under certain circumstances tolerances are permissible in the quantity of goods. See UCPDC Art. 39 b.

Rail waybill

Freight document that indicates goods have been received for shipment by rail. A duplicate is given to the shipper as a receipt for acceptance of the goods (also called duplicate waybill). See UCPDC Art. 28.

Reasonable care in advising of documentary credits

The advising bank is required to take reasonable care to check the apparent authenticity of the documentary credit which it advises. See UCPDC Art. 7.

Reasonable care in examining the documents (by the bank)

The bank must examine all stipulated documents with reasonable care to determine whether or not they appear on their face to be in compliance with the terms and conditions of the documentary credit. The documents may not be inconsistent with one another. Banks do not assume any liability or responsibility for the form, sufficiency, accuracy, genuineness, falsification, or legal effect of any documents nor do they assume any liability or responsibility for the description, quantity, weight, quality, condition, packing, delivery, value, or existence of the goods represented by any documents. See UCPDC Art. 13 and 15.

Received for shipment bill of lading

Confirms only receipt of the goods but not their actual loading on board. This type of bill of lading can be accepted under documentary credits only if this is expressly permitted or if the credit stipulates a document covering multimodal transport. Otherwise, "received for shipment" bills of lading must show an additional "On board" notation in order to be accepted as an ocean bill of lading. See UCPDC Art. 23 a ii.

Recourse

In documentary transactions the negotiating bank reserves the right of recourse to the presenter of the documents if the issuing bank does not reimburse it, provided that the negotiating bank has not confirmed the credit.

Red clause letter of credit

Clauses in letters of credit which allow advances to the beneficiary prior to the shipment of goods. The wording of the clauses stipulates the conditions of such advances.

Refusal of confirmation

An advising bank has the right to refuse the request by the issuing bank to add its confirmation to the documentary credit but must advise the issuing bank of its decision. Unless otherwise stated, it may advise the credit to the beneficiary without adding its confirmation. See UCPDC Art. 9 c i. + ii.

Refusal to accept documents

If the issuing, confirming, or nominated bank, following examination, decides to refuse the documents, it must inform the presenter without delay, but not later than seven bank working days following receipt of the documents. See UCPDC Art. 13 and 14.

Reimbursing bank

The bank named in the documentary credit from which the paying, accepting, or negotiating bank may request cover after receipt of the documents in compliance with the documentary credit. The reimbursing bank usually does not have a commitment to pay unless it has confirmed the reimbursement instruction. The issuing bank is not released from its commitment to pay through the nomination of a reimbursing bank. If cover from the reimbursing bank should not arrive in time, the issuing bank is obliged to pay (also any accrued interest on arrears). See UCPDC Art. 19.

Release of goods

Goods are often consigned to the bank of the importer/buyer. In order that these shipments can be delivered to the importer/buyer, the bank instructs the forwarder/carrier accordingly. In such cases, the importer/buyer should be aware of his obligation to honour the relative documents when presented.

Restricted letter of credit

Documentary credit where availability is restricted to a designated bank.

Revocable (documentary credit)

Revocable documentary credits must be clearly marked by the issuing bank. They may be revoked at any time until their utilization (see under "Availability under documentary credits"). Due to the low level of security they are extremely rare in practice. See UCPDC Art. 6 and 8.

Revolving documentary credit

With a revolving documentary credit the issuing bank undertakes to reinstate the credit after each drawing or time period (e.g. monthly). The number of utilizations and the period of time within which these must take place are specified in the documentary credit. The revolving documentary credit is used when a purchaser wishes to have certain partial quantities of the ordered goods delivered at specified intervals (multiple delivery contract) and when multiple documents are presented for this purpose. Such credit may be cumulative or non-cumulative.

Risk of loss in transit (of documentary credit documents)

Risk of loss or delay of documents, letters, small packages, etc. in transit.

If a documentary credit is available at the issuing bank, the beneficiary of the documentary credit (exporter) bears the risk of loss in transit of the documents to the counters of the issuing bank. This also applies even if the documents are forwarded via the advising bank. Possible consequences:

- costs for preparing duplicates
- delays in payment
- expiry of the period for presentation of documents (loss of payment under the documentary credit)

The exporter can exclude this risk by requiring the documentary credit to be available for payment, negotiation, or acceptance at the counters of the advising bank.

Said to contain (s.t.c.)/said to weigh (s.t.w.)/shipper's load and count

Clauses in transport documents which exclude liability of the carrier for the consistency of the description of the goods or the weight of the goods actually loaded, e.g. goods in containers. This provides protection to the carrier against claims by the consignee. See UCPDC Arc. 31 ii.

Sea Waybill

Transport document which is not a document of title/negotiable document. The sea waybill indicates the "on board" loading of the goods and can be used in cases where no ocean bill of lading, i.e. no document of title is required. For receipt of the goods, presentation of the sea waybill by the consignee named therein is not required, which can speed up processing at the port of destination. See UCPDC Art. 24.

Please note the disposal and cargo control provisions of this type of document.

Short drawings (of the documentary credit amount)

The UCPDC applies the procedures for partial drawings in a documentary credit. See UCPDC Art. 39.

Short form of transport documents

Transport documents which do not contain all of the conditions of the contract of carriage and/or refer to such conditions as being contained in a source document other than the transport document.

Signatures on documents

According to the UCPDC, documents may be signed by handwriting, by facsimile signature, by perforated signature, by stamp, by symbol, or by any other mechanical or electronic method of authentication. Please note, however, that documentary credits may abrogate this regulation by expressly stipulating a particular method of authentication. See UCPDC Art. 20 b.

Silent confirmation (of documentary credits)

In addition to the commitment of the issuing bank the advising bank can, by silent confirmation, enter into its own, independent commitment to pay or accept. In contrast to the confirmed documentary credit, in this case there is no confirmation instruction given by the issuing bank. Silent confirmations are thus purely agreements between the beneficiary and the "silently confirming" bank. In order to enforce its claim, the "silently confirming" bank requires the assignment of the rights of the beneficiary under the letter of credit.

Soft clause

Clauses in the documentary credit which make it impossible for the beneficiary (seller) to meet the conditions of the documentary credit on his own and independently of the purchaser.
Example:
The goods must be accepted prior to shipment by a representative of the purchaser. The name of the representative is made known via an amendment in the documentary credit at a later stage. It is not recommended for exporters to agree to this type of request.

Standby letter of credit

The standby letter of credits is very similar in nature to a guarantee. The beneficiary can claim in the event that the principal does not comply with its obligations to the beneficiary. Payment can usually be realized against presentation of a sight draft and written statement that the principal has failed to fulfil his obligations.
With this instrument the following payments and performances, among others, can be supported:
- repay funds borrowed or advanced
- fulfil subcontracts
- undertake payment of invoices made on open account.
Standby letters of credit are subject to the UCPDC.

Straight bill of lading

Bill of lading consigned to a specific party and which may not be transferred by endorsement.

Subsidiary (for transport insurances)

The goods are covered for the same period or journey and against the same dangers with two insurers. The non-contractual transport insurer has secondary liability, i.e. compensates only for damages not covered by the other insurance.

Third party documents

In documentary operations, documents which indicate as the consignor of the goods a party other than the beneficiary of the credit are referred to as "third party documents." See UCPDC Art. 31 iii.

Through bills of lading

Bills of lading where transhipment takes place en route but which cover the entire carriage of the goods from the port of loading to the final destination.

Tolerances (in amounts, quantities, unit prices)

The UCPDC stipulate the tolerances allowed with regard to amounts, quantities, and prices in documentary transactions. See UCPDC Art. 39.

Transfer risk

Currency measures of foreign governments which make it impossible for the debtor to allocate and transfer foreign exchange abroad. Transfer risks can be covered through use of bank guarantees, confirmed documentary credits, export credit agencies, etc.

Transferable (letter of credit)

In the case of a transferable documentary credit, the beneficiary named therein may request the issuing or nominated bank to transfer all or part of the documentary credit to another beneficiary. A credit can only be transferred if it is expressly designated as "transferable" by the issuing bank. This type of documentary credit enables intermediaries (first beneficiaries) to offer security in the form of documentary credits to their suppliers (second beneficiaries). See UCPDC Art. 48.

Transhipment (in documentary credits)

Even if the documentary credit prohibits transhipment, banks will accept bills of lading/sea waybills which indicate that transhipment may or will occur, provided that according to the bill of lading/sea waybill the goods were transported in containers, trailers, or LASH barges and that the entire journey is covered by a single bill of lading. In all other transport documents except charted party bills of lading and courier and post receipts, transhipment is allowed even if the documentary credit prohibits it, provided that the entire transport route is covered by a single document. See UCPDC Art. 23 b c d.

Transferable documentary credit

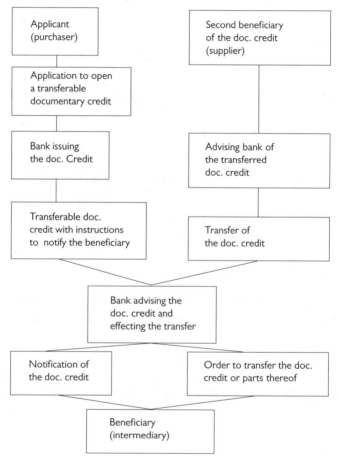

Transport documents

All types of documents evidencing shipment or dispatch of goods. Examples: bill of lading, air waybill, rail waybill, etc.

As per the ICC, forwarders certificates of receipt (FCR) and forwarders certificates of transport (FCT) are not considered transport documents and are therefore governed by UCPDC Art. 21.

UCPDC

Uniform Customs and Practice for Documentary Credits. The version valid as of 1.1.1994 is the 1993 revision, brochure no.500, of the International Chamber of Commerce in Paris.

Please ensure that the documentary credits opened in your favour are expressly subject to the UCPDC. The UCPDC is binding for all parties and covers documentary credits and standby credits. See Chapter 7 for the complete text of UCPDC 500.

Unclear, incomplete expressions/conditions/instructions

In the case of unclear instructions in documentary credits the advising bank will seek clarification from the issuing bank. The advising bank can provide the beneficiary with a preliminary copy of the documentary credit for his/her information. Formal advice follows after the unclear terms have been clarified. See UCPDC Art. 12.

Unconfirmed (documentary credit)

The issuing bank does not require confirmation of the documentary credit by the advising bank. The advising bank therefore makes no commitment to pay, accept or negotiate. See UCPDC Art. 7. See also under "Silent confirmation."

Underwriter (in connection with insurances)

Authorized signatory of an insurance company. Known primarily on the British Lloyd's insurance market, where brokers offer the underwriter risks with whom they negotiate the conditions.

Usance draft

Term in the Anglo-American areas for a term draft.

Usance letters of credit

Documentary credit which are not available by sight payment and which are therefore available against
- acceptance of a term bill of exchange
- or in certain usages by deferred payment.

Validity/expiry (of a documentary credit)

The expiry date represents the last day on which the beneficiary may present documents under the documentary credit to the nominated back.

All documentary credits must stipulate both the place and date of expiry. See also under "Latest date for presentation." See UCPDC Art. 42.

Epilogue

INTERNET AND INTERNATIONAL TRADE

The past, the present and the future are really one — they are today.

— Stowe

As the fax machine surpassed the telex machine, which traders were dependent upon for many years, so is e-mail currently replacing the fax machine. Communicating with each other through the World Wide Web is becoming a standard. Companies that are not yet utilizing the Internet for marketing their products may be losing ground to their competitors who have already discovered how to use the Internet for communication between themselves and their clients.

Continental Commodity Exchange, "WWW.CCEX.ORG", has been developed for export/import companies, trading houses, producers, and agents active in international trade. The Continental Commodity Exchange (CCE) is an international trade network of manufacturers and distributors all over the world that facilitates the trading of real goods through the World Wide Web. Suppliers can increase the sales and exposure of their goods to the global market by listing their products on the Exchange. For trading houses and import/export companies, the CCE is a vehicle for sourcing products made easy. Instead of looking through various trade directories or calling trade representatives of countries where one may think the product is manufactured, the buyer must only enter the CCE Internet site to find pertinent information at his or her fingertips.

The Continental web site sets out categories of products available in a hexagon bitmap, allowing the user to "point and click" to the desired product. Once an interest is established in a particular item, CCE provides detailed information and a picture, together with a request form. With Continental Commodity Exchange, traders no longer need to spend money and time on long-distance faxes and phone calls to obtain product information and pricing. Continental Commodity Exchange answers most questions about the product directly on the web page and allows trading of products offered by a variety of companies on a global scale.

The wireless twenty-first century is upon us. It is important to keep up with the latest changes in technology. Most banks already offer electronic banking and some banks are starting to offer electronic advising and negotiation services for documentary credits and guarantees via the Internet or through a dedicated dial-up line. For large and midsize companies handling a large volume of documents such services may prove to be very efficient. Do not get left behind. Make the technology work for you and take the future into your own hands.